THE SEQUEL OF APPOMATTOX

EXTRA-ILLUSTRATED EDITION

∴

VOLUME 32
THE CHRONICLES
OF AMERICA SERIES

ALLEN JOHNSON
EDITOR

GERHARD R. LOMER
CHARLES W. JEFFERYS
ASSISTANT EDITORS

Gravure, Andersen-Lamb Co. N.Y.

CHARLES SUMNER

Photograph by J. W. Black and Co., Boston.   In the collections of
the Bostonian Society, Old State House, Boston.

THE SEQUEL
OF APPOMATTOX

A CHRONICLE OF THE
REUNION OF THE STATES
BY WALTER LYNWOOD FLEMING

NEW HAVEN: YALE UNIVERSITY PRESS
TORONTO: GLASGOW, BROOK & CO.
LONDON: HUMPHREY MILFORD
OXFORD UNIVERSITY PRESS
1921

Copyright, 1919, by Yale University Press

CONTENTS

CONTENTS

ILLUSTRATIONS

ix

THE SEQUEL OF APPOMATTOX

∴

CHAPTER I

THE AFTERMATH OF WAR

WHEN the armies of the Union and of the Confederacy were disbanded in 1865, two matters had been settled beyond further dispute: the negro was to be free, and the Union was to be perpetuated. But though slavery and state sovereignty were no longer at issue, there were still many problems which pressed for solution. The huge task of reconstruction must be faced. The nature of the situation required that the measures of reconstruction be first formulated in Washington by the victors and then worked out in the conquered South. Since the success of these policies would depend in a large measure upon their acceptability to both sections of the country, it was expected that the North would be influenced to some extent by the attitude of the Southern people, which in turn would be determined largely by local conditions in the South. The situation in the South at the close of the Civil War is therefore the point at which this narrative of the reconstruction naturally takes its beginning.

The surviving Confederate soldiers came straggling back to communities which were now far from being satisfactory dwelling places for civilized people. Everywhere they found missing many of the best of their former neighbors. They found property destroyed, the labor system disorganized, and the inhabitants in many places suffering from want. They found the white people demoralized and sometimes divided among themselves, and the negroes free, bewildered, and disorderly, for organized government had lapsed with the surrender of the Confederate armies.

Beneath a disorganized society lay a devastated land. The destruction of property affected all classes of the population. The accumulated capital of the South had disappeared in worthless Confederate stocks, bonds, and currency. The banks had failed early in the war. Two billion dollars invested in slaves had been wiped out. Factories which had been running before the war, or were developed after 1861 in order to supply the blockaded country, had been destroyed by Federal raiders or seized and sold or dismantled because they had furnished supplies to the Confederacy. Mining industries were paralyzed. Public buildings which had been used for war purposes were destroyed or confiscated for the uses of the army or for the new freedmen's schools. It was months before courthouses, state capitols, school and college buildings were again made available for normal uses. The military school buildings had been destroyed by the Federal forces. Among the schools which suffered were the Virginia Military Institute, the University of Alabama, the Louisiana State Seminary, and many smaller institutions. Nearly all these had been used in some way for war purposes and were therefore subject to destruction or confiscation.

The farmers and planters found themselves "land poor." The soil remained, but there was a prevalent lack of labor, of agricultural equipment, of farm stock, of seeds, and of money with which to make good the deficiency. As a result, a man with hundreds of acres might be as poor as a negro refugee. The desolation is thus described by a Virginia farmer:

From Harper's Ferry to New Market, which is about eighty miles . . . the country was almost a desert. . . . We had no cattle, hogs, sheep, or horse or anything else. The fences were all gone. Some of the orchards were very much injured, but the fruit trees had not been destroyed. The barns were all burned; chimneys standing without houses, and houses standing without roof, or door, or window.

Much land was thrown on the market at low prices—three to five dollars an acre for land worth fifty dollars. The poorer lands could not be sold at all, and thousands of farms were deserted by their owners. Everywhere recovery from this agricultural depression was slow. Five years after the war Robert Somers, an English traveler, said of the Tennessee Valley:

It consists for the most part of plantations in a state of semi-ruin and plantations of which the ruin is for the present total and complete. . . . The trail of war is visible throughout the valley in burnt-up gin-houses, ruined bridges, mills, and factories . . . and in large tracts of once cultivated land stripped of every vestige of fencing. The roads, long neglected, are in disorder, and having in many places become impassable, new tracks have been made through the woods and fields without much respect to boundaries.

Similar conditions existed wherever the armies had passed, and not in the country districts alone.

Many of the cities, such as Richmond, Charleston, Columbia, Jackson, Atlanta, and Mobile had suffered from fire or bombardment.

There were few stocks of merchandise in the South when the war ended, and Northern creditors had lost so heavily through the failure of Southern merchants that they were cautious about extending credit again. Long before 1865 all coin had been sent out in contraband trade through the blockade. That there was a great need of supplies from the outside world is shown by the following statement of General Boynton:

Window-glass has given way to thin boards, in railway coaches and in the cities. Furniture is marred and broken, and none has been replaced for four years. Dishes are cemented in various styles, and half the pitchers have tin handles. A complete set of crockery is never seen, and in very few families is there enough to set a table. . . . A set of forks with whole tines is a curiosity. Clocks and watches have nearly all stopped. . . . Hair brushes and tooth brushes have all worn out; combs are broken. . . . Pins, needles, and thread, and a thousand such articles, which seem indispensable to housekeeping, are very scarce. Even in weaving on the looms, corncobs have been substituted for spindles. Few have pocket knives. In fact, everything that has heretofore been an article of sale at the South is wanting now. At the tables of those who were once esteemed luxurious providers you will find neither tea, coffee, sugar, nor spices of any kind. Even candles, in some cases, have been replaced by a cup of grease in which a piece of cloth is plunged for a wick.

This poverty was prolonged and rendered more acute by the lack of transportation. Horses, mules, wagons, and carriages were scarce, the country roads were nearly impassable, and bridges were in bad repair or had been burned or washed away. Steamboats had almost disappeared from the rivers. Those which had escaped capture as blockade runners had been subsequently destroyed or were worn out. Postal facilities, which had been poor enough during the last year of the Confederacy, were entirely lacking for several months after the surrender.

The railways were in a state of physical dilapidation little removed from destruction, save for those that had been captured and kept in partial repair by the Federal troops. The rolling stock had been lost by capture, by destruction to prevent capture, in wrecks, which were frequent, or had been worn out. The railroad companies possessed large sums in Confederate currency and in securities which were now valueless. About two-thirds of all the lines were hopelessly bankrupt. Fortunately the United States War Department took over the control of the railway lines and in some cases effected a temporary reorganization which could not have been accomplished by the bankrupt companies. During the summer and fall of 1865 "loyal" boards of directors were appointed for most of the roads, and the army withdrew its control. But repairs and reconstruction were accomplished with difficulty because of the demoralization of labor and the lack of funds or credit. Freight was scarce and, had it not been for government shipments, some of the roads would have been abandoned. Not many people were able to travel. It is recorded that on one trip from Montgomery to Mobile and return, a distance of 360 miles, the road which is now the Louisville and Nashville collected only thirteen dollars in fares.

Had there been unrestricted commercial freedom in the South in 1865–66, the distress of the people would have been somewhat lessened, for here and there were to be found public and private stores of cotton, tobacco, rice, and other farm products, all of which were bringing high prices in the market. But for several months the operation of wartime laws and regulations hindered the distribution of even these scanty stores. Property upon which the Confederate Government had a claim was of course subject to confiscation, and private property offered for sale, even that of Unionists, was subject to a 25 per cent tax on sales, a shipping tax, and a revenue tax. The revenue tax on cotton, ranging from two to three cents a pound during the three years after the war, brought in over $68,000,000. This tax, with other Federal revenues, yielded much more than the entire expenses of reconstruction from 1865 to 1868 and of all relief measures for the South, both public and private. After May, 1865, the 25 per cent tax was imposed only upon the produce of slave labor. None of the war taxes, except that on cotton, was levied upon the crops of 1866, but while these taxes lasted they seriously impeded the resumption of trade.

Even these restrictions, however, might have been borne if only they had been honestly applied. Unfortunately, some of the most spectacular frauds ever perpetrated were carried through in connection with the attempt of the United States Treasury Department to collect and sell the confiscable property in the South. The property to be sold consisted of what had been captured and seized by the army and the navy, of "abandoned" property, as such was called whose owner was absent in the Confederate service, and of property subject to seizure under the confiscation acts of Congress. No captures were made after the general surrender, and no further seizures of "abandoned" property were made after Johnson's amnesty proclamation of May 29, 1865. This left only the "confiscable" property to be collected and sold.

For collection purposes the States of the South were divided into districts, each under the supervision of an agent of the Treasury Department, who received a commission of about 25 per cent. Cotton, regarded as the root of the slavery evil, was singled out as the principal object of confiscation. It was known that the Confederate Government had owned in 1865 about 150,000 bales, but the records were defective and much of it, with no clear indication of ownership, still remained with the producers. Secretary Chase, foreseeing the difficulty of effecting a just settlement, counseled against seizure, but his judgment was overruled. Secretary McCulloch said of his agents: "I am sure I sent some honest cotton agents South; but it sometimes seems doubtful whether any of them remained honest very long." Some of the natives, even, became cotton thieves. In a report made in 1866, McCulloch describes their methods:

Contractors, anxious for gain, were sometimes guilty of bad faith and peculation, and frequently took possession of cotton and delivered it under contracts as captured or abandoned, when in fact it was not such, and they had no right to touch it. . . . Residents and others in the districts where these peculations were going on took advantage of the unsettled condition of the country, and representing themselves as agents of this department, went about robbing under such pretended authority, and thus added to the difficulties of the situation by causing unjust opprobrium and suspicion to rest upon officers engaged in the faithful discharge of their duties. Agents, . . . frequently received or collected property, and sent it forward which the law did not authorize them to take. . . . Lawless men, singly and in organized bands, engaged in general plunder; every species of intrigue and peculation and theft were resorted to.

These agents turned over to the United States about $34,000,000. About 40,000 claimants were subsequently indemnified on the ground that the property taken from them did not belong to the Confederate Government, but many thousands of other claimants have been unable to prove that their property was seized by government agents and hence have received nothing. It is probable that the actual Confederate property was nearly all stolen by the agents. One agent in Alabama sold an appointment as assistant for $25,000, and a few months later both the assistant and the agent were tried by a military court for stealing and were fined \$90,000 and \$250,000 respectively in addition to being imprisoned.

Other property, including horses, mules, wagons, tobacco, rice, and sugar which the natives claimed as their own, was seized. In some places the agents even collected delinquent Confederate taxes. Much of the confiscable property was not sold but was turned over to the Freedmen's Bureau[1] for its support. The total amount seized cannot be satisfactorily ascertained. The Ku Klux minority report asserted that 3,000,000 bales of cotton were taken, of which the United States received only 114,000. It is certain that, owing to the deliberate destruction of cotton by fire in 1864–65, this estimate was too high, but all the testimony points to the fact that the frauds were stupendous. As a result the United States Government did not succeed in obtaining the Confederate property to which it had a claim, and the country itself was stripped of necessities to a degree that left it not only destitute but outraged and embittered. "Such practices," said Trowbridge, "had a pernicious effect, engendering a contempt for the Government and a murderous

[1] See pp. 89 *et seq.*

ill-will which too commonly vented itself upon soldiers and negroes."

The South faced the work of reconstruction not only with a shortage of material and greatly hampered in the employment even of that but still more with a shortage of men. The losses among the whites are usually estimated at about half the military population, but since accurate records are lacking the exact numbers cannot be ascertained. The best of the civil leaders, as well as the prominent military leaders, had so committed themselves to the support of the Confederacy as to be excluded from participation in any reconstruction that might be attempted. The business of reconstruction, therefore, fell of necessity to the Confederate private soldiers, the lower officers, nonparticipants, and lukewarm individuals who had not greatly compromised themselves. These politically and physically uninjured survivors included also all the "slackers" of the Confederacy. But though there were such physical and moral losses on the part of those to whom fell the direction of affairs there was also a moral strengthening in the sound element of the people who had been tried by the discipline of war.

The greatest weakness of both races was their

extreme poverty.   The crops of 1865 turned out badly, for most of the soldiers reached home too late for successful planting and the negro labor was not dependable.   The sale of such cotton and farm products as had escaped the treasury agents was of some help, but curiously enough much of the good money thus obtained was spent extravagantly by a people used to Confederate rag money and for four years deprived of the luxuries of life. The poorer whites who had lost all were close to starvation.   In the white counties which had sent so large a proportion of men to the army the destitution was most acute.   In many families the breadwinner had been killed in war.   After 1862 relief systems had been organized in nearly all the Confederate States for the purpose of aiding the poor whites, but these organizations were disbanded in 1865.   A Freedmen's Bureau official traveling through the desolate back country furnishes a description which might have applied to two hundred counties, a third of the South: "It is a common, an every-day sight in Randolph County, that of women and children, most of whom were formerly in good circumstances, begging for bread from door to door.   Meat of any kind has been a stranger to many of their mouths for months.   The drought cut off what little crops they hoped to save, and they must have immediate help or perish.   By far the greater suffering exists among the whites.   Their scanty supplies have been exhausted, and now they look to the Government alone for support.   Some are without homes of any description."

Where the armies had passed, few of the people, white or black, remained; most of them had been forced as "refugees" within the Union lines or into the interior of the Confederacy.   Now, along with the disbanded Confederate soldiers, they came straggling back to their war-swept homes.   It was estimated, in December, 1865, that in the States of Alabama, Mississippi, and Georgia, there were five hundred thousand white people who were without the necessaries of life; numbers died from lack of food.   Within a few months relief agencies were at work.   In the North, especially in the border States and in New York, charitable organizations collected and forwarded great quantities of supplies to the negroes and to the whites in the hill and mountain counties.   The reorganized state and local governments sent food from the unravaged portions of the Black Belt to the nearest white counties, and the army commanders gave some

aid. As soon as the Freedmen's Bureau was organized, it fed to the limit of its supplies the needy
whites as well as the blacks.

The extent of the relief afforded by the charity
of the North and by the agencies of the United
States Government is not now generally remembered, probably on account of the later objectionable activities of the Freedmen's Bureau, but it
was at the time properly appreciated. A Southern
journalist, writing of what he saw in Georgia,
remarked that "it must be a matter of gratitude
as well as surprise for our people to see a Government which was lately fighting us with fire and
sword and shell, now generously feeding our poor
and distressed. In the immense crowds which
throng the distributing house, I notice the mothers
and fathers, widows and orphans of our soldiers.
. . . Again, the Confederate soldier, with one leg
or one arm, the crippled, maimed, and broken, and
the worn and destitute men, who fought bravely
their enemies then, their benefactors now, have
their sacks filled and are fed."

Acute distress continued until 1867; after that
year there was no further danger of starvation.
Some of the poor whites, especially in the remote districts, never again reached a comfortable standard

of living; some were demoralized by too much assistance; others were discouraged and left the South for the West or the North. But the mass of the people accepted the discipline of poverty and made the best of their situation.

The difficulties, however, that beset even the courageous and the competent were enormous. The general paralysis of industry, the breaking up of society, and poverty on all sides bore especially hard on those who had not previously been manual laborers. Physicians could get practice enough but no fees; lawyers who had supported the Confederacy found it difficult to get back into the reorganized courts because of the test oaths and the competition of "loyal" attorneys; and for the teachers there were few schools. We read of officers high in the Confederate service selling to Federal soldiers the pies and cakes cooked by their wives, of others selling fish and oysters which they themselves had caught, and of men and women hitching themselves to plows when they had no horse or mule.

Such incidents must, from their nature, have been infrequent, but they show to what straits some at least were reduced. Six years after the war, James S. Pike, then in South Carolina, mentions cases which might be duplicated in nearly every old Southern community: "In the vicinity," he says, "lived a gentleman whose income when the war broke out was rated at $150,000 a year. Not a vestige of his whole vast estate remains today. Not far distant were the estates of a large proprietor and a well known family, rich and distinguished for generations. The slaves were gone. The family is gone. A single scion of the house remains, and he peddles tea by the pound and molasses by the quart, on a corner of the old homestead, to the former slaves of the family and thereby earns his livelihood."

General Lee's good example influenced many. Commercial enterprises were willing to pay for the use of his name and reputation, but he wished to farm and could get no opportunity. "They are offering my father everything," his daughter said, "except the only thing he will accept, a place to earn honest bread while engaged in some useful work." This remark led to an offer of the presidency of Washington College, now Washington and Lee University, which he accepted. "I have a self-imposed task which I must accomplish," he said, "I have led the young men of the South in battle; I have seen many of them fall under my

2

standard. I shall devote my life now to training young men to do their duty in life."

The condition of honest folk was still further troubled by a general spirit of lawlessness in many regions. Virginia, Tennessee, Arkansas, and Louisiana recognized the "Union" state government, but the coming of peace brought legal anarchy to the other States of the Confederacy. The Confederate state and local governments were abolished as the armies of occupation spread over the South, and for a period of four or six months there was no government except that exercised by the commanders of the military garrisons left behind when the armies marched away. Even before the surrender the local governments were unable to make their authority respected, and soon after the war ended parts of the country became infested with outlaws, pretended treasury agents, horse thieves, cattle thieves, and deserters. Away from the military posts only lynch law could cope with these elements of disorder. With the aid of the army in the more settled regions, and by extra-legal means elsewhere, the outlaws, thieves, cotton burners, and house burners were brought somewhat under control even before the state governments were reorganized, though the embers of lawlessness continued to smolder.

The relations between the Federal soldiers stationed in the principal towns and the native white population were not, on the whole, so bad as might have been expected. If the commanding officer were well disposed, there was little danger of friction, though sometimes his troops got out of hand. The regulars had a better reputation than the volunteers. The Confederate soldiers were surfeited with fighting, but the "stay-at-home" element was often a cause of trouble. The problem of social relations between the conquerors and the conquered was troublesome. The men might get along well together, but the women would have nothing do with the "Yankees" and ill feeling arose because of their antipathy. Carl Schurz reported that "the soldier of the Union is looked upon as a stranger, an intruder, as the 'Yankee,' the 'enemy.' . . . The existence and intensity of this aversion is too well known to those who have served or are serving in the South to require proof."

In retaliation the soldiers developed ingenious ways of annoying the whites. Women, forced for any reason to go to headquarters, were made to take the oath of allegiance or the "ironclad" oath before their requests were granted; flags were fastened over doors, gates, or sidewalks in order to irritate the recalcitrant dames and their daughters. Confederate songs and color combinations were forbidden. In Richmond, General Halleck ordered that no marriages be performed unless the bride, the groom, and the officiating clergyman took the oath of allegiance. He explained this as a measure taken to prevent "the propagation of legitimate rebels."

The wearing of Confederate uniforms was forbidden by military order, but by May, 1865, few soldiers possessed regulation uniforms. In Tennessee the State also imposed fines upon wearers of the uniform. In the vicinity of military posts buttons and marks of rank were usually ordered removed and the gray clothes dyed with some other color. General Lee, for example, had the buttons on his coat covered with cloth. But frequently the Federal commander, after issuing the orders, paid no more attention to the matter and such conflicts as arose on account of the uniform were usually caused by officious enlisted men and the negro troops. Whitelaw Reid relates the following incident:

Nothing was more touching, in all that I saw in Savannah, than the almost painful effort of the rebels, from generals down to privates, to conduct themselves so as to evince respect for our soldiers, and to bring no severer punishment upon the city than it had already received.   There was a brutal scene at the hotel, where a drunken sergeant, with a pair of tailor's shears, insisted on cutting the buttons from the uniform of an elegant gray-headed old brigadier, who had just come in from Johnston's army; but he bore himself modestly and very handsomely through it.   His staff was composed of fine-looking, stalwart fellows, evidently gentlemen, who appeared intensely mortified at such treatment.   They had no clothes except their rebel uniforms, and had, as yet, had no time to procure others, but they avoided disturbances and submitted to what they might, with some propriety, and with the general approval of our officers, have resented.

The negro troops, even at their best, were everywhere considered offensive by the native whites. General Grant, indeed, urged that only white troops be used to garrison the interior.   But the negro soldier, impudent by reason of his new freedom, his new uniform, and his new gun, was more than Southern temper could tranquilly bear, and race conflicts were frequent.   A New Orleans newspaper thus states the Southern point of view: "Our citizens who had been accustomed to meet and treat the negroes only as respectful servants, were mortified, pained, and shocked to encounter them . . . wearing Federal uniforms and bearing bright muskets and gleaming bayonets. . . . They are jostled from the sidewalks by dusky guards, marching four abreast. They were halted, in rude and sullen tones, by negro sentinels."

The task of the Federal forces was not easy. The garrisons were not large enough nor numerous enough to keep order in the absence of civil government. The commanders in the South asked in vain for cavalry to police the rural districts. Much of the disorder, violence, and incendiarism attributed at the time to lawless soldiers appeared later to be due to discharged soldiers and others pretending to be soldiers in order to carry out schemes of robbery. The whites complained vigorously of the garrisons, and petitions were sent to Washington from mass meetings and from state legislatures asking for their removal. The higher commanders, however, bore themselves well, and in a few fortunate cases Southern whites were on most amicable terms with the garrison commanders. The correspondence of responsible military officers in the South shows how earnestly and considerately each, as a rule, tried to work out his task. The good sense of most of the Federal officers appeared when, after the murder of Lincoln, even General Grant for a brief space lost his head and ordered the arrest of paroled Confederates.

The church organizations were as much involved in the war and in the reconstruction as were secular institutions. Before the war every religious organization having members North and South, except the Catholic Church and the Jews, had separated into independent Northern and Southern bodies. In each section church feeling ran high, and when the war came the churches supported the armies. As the Federal armies occupied Southern territory, the church buildings of each denomination were turned over to the corresponding Northern body, and Southern ministers were permitted to remain only upon agreeing to conduct "loyal services, pray for the President of the United States and for Federal victories" and to foster "loyal sentiment." The Protestant Episcopal churches in Alabama were closed from September to December, 1865, and some congregations were dispersed by the soldiers because Bishop Wilmer had directed his clergy to omit the prayer for President Davis but had substituted no other. The ministers of non-liturgical churches were not so easily controlled. A Georgia Methodist preacher directed by a Federal officer to pray for the President said afterwards: "I prayed for the President that the Lord would take out of him and his allies the hearts of beasts and put into them the hearts of men or remove the cusses from office." Sometimes members of a congregation showed their resentment at the "loyal" prayers by leaving the church. But in spite of many irritations both sides frequently managed to get some amusement out of the "loyal" services. The church situation was, however, a serious matter during and after the reconstruction, and some of its later phases will have to be discussed elsewhere.

The Unionist, or "Tory," of the lower and eastern South found himself, in 1865, a man without a country. Few in number in any community, they found themselves upon their return from a harsh exile the victims of ostracism or open hostility. One of them, William H. Smith, later Governor of Alabama, testified that the Southern people "manifest the most perfect contempt for a man who is known to be an unequivocal Union man; they call him a 'galvanized Yankee' and apply other terms and epithets to him." General George H. Thomas, speaking of a region more divided in sentiment than Alabama, remarked that "Middle Tennessee is disturbed by animosities and hatreds, much more than it is by the disloyalty of persons towards the Government of the United States.

Those personal animosities would break out and overawe the civil authorities, but for the presence there of the troops of the United States. . . . They are more unfriendly to Union men, natives of the State of Tennessee, or of the South, who have been in the Union army, than they are to men of Northern birth."

In the border States society was sharply divided and feeling was bitter. In eastern Tennessee, eastern Kentucky, West Virginia, and parts of Arkansas and Missouri returning Confederates met harsher treatment than did the Unionists in the lower South. Trowbridge says of east Tennessee: "Returning rebels were robbed; and if one had stolen unawares to his home, it was not safe for him to remain there. I saw in Virginia one of these exiles, who told me how homesickly he pined for the hills and meadows of east Tennessee, which he thought the most delightful region in the world. But there was a rope hanging from a tree for him there, and he dared not go back. 'The bottom rails are on top,' said he, 'that is the trouble.' The Union element, and the worst part of the Union element, was uppermost." Confederates and Confederate sympathizers in Maryland, West Virginia, Tennessee, and Kentucky were disfranchised. In West Virginia, Tennessee, and Missouri "war trespass" suits were brought against returning Confederates for military acts done in war time. In Missouri and West Virginia strict test oaths excluded Confederates from office, from the polls, and from the professions of teaching, preaching, and law. On the other hand in central and western Kentucky the predominant Unionist population, themselves suffering through the abolition of slavery, and by the objectionable operations of the Freedmen's Bureau and the unwise military administration, showed more sympathy for the Confederates, welcomed them home, and soon relieved them of all restrictions.

Still another element of discord was added by the Northerners who came to exploit the South. Many mustered-out soldiers proposed to stay. Speculators of all kinds followed the withdrawing Confederate lines and with the conclusion of peace spread through the country; but they were not cordially received. With the better class, the Southerners, especially the soldiers, associated freely if seldom intimately. But the conduct of a few of their number who considered that the war had opened all doors to them, who very freely expressed their views, gave advice, condemned old customs, and were generally offensive, did much to bring all Northerners into disrepute. Tactlessly critical letters published in Northern papers did not add to their popularity. The few Northern women felt the ostracism more keenly than did the men. Benjamin C. Truman, an agent of President Johnson, thus summed up the situation: "There is a prevalent disposition not to associate too freely with Northern men or to receive them into the circles of society; but it is far from unsurmountable. Over Southern society, as over every other, woman reigns supreme, and they are more embittered against those whom they deem the authors of all their calamities than are their brothers, sons, and husbands." But of the thousands of Northern men who overcame the reluctance of the Southerners to social intercourse little was heard. Many a Southern planter secured a Northern partner, or sold him half his plantation to get money to run the other half. For the irritations of 1865 each party must take its share of responsibility.

Had the South assisted in a skillful and adequate publicity, much disastrous misunderstanding might have been avoided. The North knew as little of the South as the South did of the North, but the North was eager for news. Able newspaper correspondents like Sidney Andrews of the Boston *Advertiser* and the Chicago *Tribune*, who opposed President Johnson's policies, Thomas W. Knox of the New York *Herald*, who had given General Sherman so much trouble in Tennessee, Whitelaw Reid, who wrote for several papers and tried cotton planting in Louisiana, and John T. Trowbridge, New England author and journalist, were dispatched southwards. Chief of the President's investigators were General Carl Schurz, German revolutionist, Federal soldier, and soon to be radical Republican, who held harsh views of the Southern people; and there were besides Harvey M. Watterson, Kentucky Democrat and Unionist, the father of "Marse" Henry; Benjamin C. Truman, New England journalist and soldier, whose long report was perhaps the best of all; Chief Justice Chase, who was thinking mainly of "How soon can the negro vote?"; and General Grant, who made a report so brief that, notwithstanding its value, it attracted little attention. In addition, a constant stream of information and misinformation was going northward from treasury agents, officers of the army, the Freedmen's Bureau, teachers, and missionaries. Among foreigners who described the conquered land were Robert

Somers, Henry Latham, and William Hepworth Dixon. But few in the South realized the importance of supplying the North with correct information about actual conditions. The letters and reports, they thought, humiliated them; inquiry was felt to be prying and gloating. "Correspondents have added a new pang to surrender," it was said. The South was proud and refused to be catechized. From the Northern point of view the South, a new and strange region, with strange customs and principles, was of course not to be considered as quite normal and American, but there was on the part of many correspondents a determined attempt to describe things as they were. And yet the North persisted in its unsympathetic queries when it seemed to have a sufficient answer in the reports of Grant, Schurz, and Truman.

Grant's opinion was short and direct: "I am satisfied that the mass of thinking men of the South accept the present situation of affairs in good faith. . . . The citizens of the Southern States are anxious to return to self-government within the Union as soon as possible." Truman came to the conclusion that "the rank and file of the disbanded Southern army . . . are the backbone and sinew of the South. . . . To the disbanded regiments of the rebel army, both officers and men, I look with great confidence as the best and altogether the most hopeful element of the South, the real basis of reconstruction and the material of worthy citizenship." General John Tarbell, before the Joint Committee on Reconstruction, testified that "there are, no doubt, disloyal and disorderly persons in the South, but it is an entire mistake to apply these terms to a whole people. I would as soon travel alone, unarmed, through the South as through the North. The South I left is not at all the South I hear and read about in the North. From the sentiment I hear in the North, I would scarcely recognize the people I saw, and, except their politics, I liked so well. I have entire faith that the better classes are friendly to the negroes."

Carl Schurz on the other hand was not so favorably impressed. "The loyalty of the masses and most of the leaders of the southern people," he said, "consists in submission to necessity. There is, except in individual instances, an entire absence of that national spirit which forms the basis of true loyalty and patriotism." Another government official in Florida was quite doubtful of the Southern whites. "I would pin them down at the point of the bayonet," he declared, "so close that they would not have room to wiggle, and allow intelligent colored people to go up and vote in preference to them. The only Union element in the South proper . . . is among the colored people. The whites will treat you very kindly to your face, but they are deceitful. I have often thought, and so expressed myself, that there is so much deception among the people of the South since the rebellion, that if an earthquake should open and swallow them up, I was fearful that the devil would be dethroned and some of them take his place."

The point of view of the Confederate military leaders was exhibited by General Wade Hampton in a letter to President Johnson and by General Lee in his advice to Governor Letcher of Virginia. General Hampton wrote: "The South unequivocally 'accepts the situation' in which she is placed. Everything that she has done has been done in perfect faith, and in the true and highest sense of the word, she is loyal. By this I mean that she intends to abide by the laws of the land honestly, to fulfill all her obligations faithfully and to keep her word sacredly, and I assert that the North has no right to demand more of her. You have no right to ask, or expect that she will at once profess unbounded love to that Union from which for four years she tried to escape at the cost of her best blood and all her treasures." General Lee in order to set an example applied through General Grant for a pardon under the amnesty proclamation and soon afterwards he wrote to Governor Letcher: "All should unite in honest efforts to obliterate the effects of war, and to restore the blessings of peace. They should remain, if possible, in the country; promote harmony and good-feeling; qualify themselves to vote; and elect to the State and general legislatures wise and patriotic men, who will devote their abilities to the interests of the country and the healing of all dissensions; I have invariably recommended this course since the cessation of hostilities, and have endeavored to practice it myself."

Southerners of the Confederacy everywhere, then, accepted the destruction of slavery and the renunciation of state sovereignty; they welcomed an early restoration of the Union, without any punishment of leaders of the defeated cause. But they were proud of their Confederate records though now legally "loyal" to the United States; they considered the negro as free but inferior, and expected to be permitted to fix his status in the social organization and to solve the problem of free labor in their own way. To embarrass the easy and permanent realization of these views there was a society disrupted, economically prostrate, deprived of its natural leaders, subjected to a control not always wisely conceived nor effectively exercised, and, finally, containing within its own population unassimilated elements which presented problems fraught with difficulty and danger.

3

CHAPTER II

WHEN FREEDOM CRIED OUT

THE negro is the central figure in the reconstruction of the South. Without the negro there would have been no Civil War. Granting a war fought for any other cause, the task of reconstruction would, without him, have been comparatively simple. With him, however, reconstruction meant more than the restoring of shattered resources; it meant the more or less successful attempt to obtain and secure for the freedman civil and political rights, and to improve his economic and social status. In 1861 the American negro was everywhere an inferior, and most of his race were slaves; in 1865 he was no longer a slave, but whether he was to be serf, ward, or citizen was an unsettled problem; in 1868 he was in the South the legal and political equal, frequently the superior, of the white; and before the end of the reconstruction period he was made by the legislation of some

States and by Congress the legal equal of the white even in certain social matters.

The race problem which confronted the American people had no parallel in the past. British and Spanish-American emancipation of slaves had affected only small numbers or small regions, in which one race greatly outnumbered the other. The results of these earlier emancipations of the negroes and the difficulties of European states in dealing with subject white populations were not such as to afford helpful example to American statesmen. But since it was the actual situation in the Southern States rather than the experience of other countries which shaped the policies adopted during reconstruction, it is important to examine with some care the conditions in which the negroes in the South found themselves at the close of the war.

The negroes were not all helpless and without experience "when freedom cried out."[1] In the Border States and in the North there were, in 1861, half a million free negroes accustomed to looking out for themselves. Nearly 200,000 negro men were enlisted in the United States army between 1862 and 1865, and many thousands of slaves had followed raiding Federal forces to freedom or had

[1] A negro phrase much used in referring to emancipation.

escaped through the Confederate lines. State emancipation in Missouri, Maryland, West Virginia,
and Tennessee, and the practical application of
the Emancipation Proclamation where the Union
armies were in control ended slavery for many
thousands more. Wherever the armies marched,
slavery ended. This was true even in Kentucky,
where the institution was not legally abolished
until the adoption of the Thirteenth Amendment.
Altogether more than a million negroes were free
and to some extent habituated to freedom before
May, 1865.

Most of these war-emancipated negroes were
scattered along the borders of the Confederacy, in
camps, in colonies, in the towns, on refugee farms,
at work with the armies, or serving as soldiers
in the ranks. There were large working colonies
along the Atlantic coast from Maryland to Florida.
The chief centers were near Norfolk, where General
Butler was the first to establish a "contraband"
camp, in North Carolina, and on the Sea Islands of
South Carolina, Georgia, and Florida, which had
been seized by the Federal fleet early in the war.
To the Sea Islands also were sent, in 1865, the
hordes of negroes who had followed General Sherman out of Georgia and South Carolina. Through

WADE HAMPTON

Photograph by H. P. Cook, Richmond, Virginia.

WADE HAMPTON

Photograph by H. P. Cook, Richmond, Virginia

Gravure Andersen-Lamb Co. N.Y.

the Border States from the Atlantic to the Mississippi and along both sides of the Mississippi from Cairo, Illinois, to New Orleans, there were other refugee camps, farms, and colonies. For periods varying from one to four years these free negroes had been at work, often amid conditions highly unfavorable to health, under the supervision of officers of the Treasury Department or of the army.

Emancipation was therefore a gradual process, and most of the negroes, through their widening experience on the plantations, with the armies, and in the colonies, were better fitted for freedom in 1865 than they had been in 1861. Even their years of bondage had done something for them, for they knew how to work and they had adopted in part the language, habits, religion, and morals of the whites. But slavery had not made them thrifty, self-reliant, or educated. Frederick Douglass said of the negro at the end of his servitude: "He had none of the conditions of self-preservation or self-protection. He was free from the individual master, but he had nothing but the dusty road under his feet. He was free from the old quarter that once gave him shelter, but a slave to the rains of summer and to the frosts of winter. He was turned loose, naked, hungry, and destitute to the open sky."

To prove that he was free the negro thought he must leave his old master, change his name, quit work for a time, perhaps get a new wife, and hang around the Federal soldiers in camp or garrison, or go to the towns where the Freedmen's Bureau was in process of organization. To the negroes who remained at home — and, curiously enough, for a time at least many did so — the news of freedom was made known somewhat ceremonially by the master or his representative. The negroes were summoned to the "big house," told that they were free, and advised to stay on for a share of the crop. The description by Mrs. Clayton, the wife of a Southern general, will serve for many: "My husband said, 'I think it best for me to inform our negroes of their freedom.' So he ordered all the grown slaves to come to him, and told them they no longer belonged to him as property, but were all free. 'You are not bound to remain with me any longer, and I have a proposition to make to you. If any of you desire to leave, I propose to furnish you with a conveyance to move you, and with provisions for the balance of the year.' The universal answer was, 'Master, we want to stay right here with you.' In many instances the slaves were so infatuated with the idea of being, as they said, 'free as birds' that they left their homes and consequently suffered; but our slaves were not so foolish."[1]

The negroes, however, had learned of their freedom before their old masters returned from the war; they were aware that the issues of the war involved in some way the question of their freedom or servitude, and through the "grape vine telegraph," the news brought by the invading soldiers, and the talk among the whites, they had long been kept fairly well informed. What the idea of freedom meant to the negroes it is difficult to say. Some thought that there would be no more work and that all would be cared for by the Government; others believed that education and opportunity were about to make them the equal of their masters. The majority of them were too bewildered to appreciate anything except the fact that they were free from enforced labor.

Conditions were most disturbed in the so-called "Black Belt," consisting of about two hundred counties in the most fertile parts of the South, where the plantation system was best developed and where by far the majority of the negroes were segregated. The negroes in the four hundred

[1] *Black and White under the Old Régime*, p. 152.

more remote and less fertile "white" counties, which had been less disturbed by armies, were not so upset by freedom as those of the Black Belt, for the garrisons and the larger towns, both centers of demoralization, were in or near the Black Belt. But there was a moving to and fro on the part of those who had escaped from the South or had been captured during the war or carried into the interior of the South to prevent capture. To those who left slavery and home to find freedom were added those who had found freedom and were now trying to get back home or to get away from the negro camps and colonies which were breaking up. A stream of immigration which began to flow to the southwest affected negroes as far as the Atlantic coast. In the confusion of moving, families were broken up, and children, wife, or husband were often lost to one another. The very old people and the young children were often left behind for the former master to care for. Regiments of negro soldiers were mustered out in every large town and their numbers were added to the disorderly mass. Some of the Federal garrisons and Bureau stations were almost overwhelmed by the numbers of blacks who settled down upon them waiting for freedom to bestow its full measure of blessing, and many of the negroes continued to remain in a demoralized condition until the new year.

The first year of freedom was indeed a year of disease, suffering, and death. Several partial censuses indicate that in 1865–66 the negro population lost as many by disease as the whites had lost in war. Ill-fed, crowded in cabins near the garrisons or entirely without shelter, and unaccustomed to caring for their own health, the blacks who were searching for freedom fell an easy prey to ordinary diseases and to epidemics. Poor health conditions prevailed for several years longer. In 1870 Robert Somers remarked that "the health of the whites has greatly improved since the war, while the health of the negroes has declined till the mortality of the colored population, greater than the mortality of the whites was before the war, has now become so markedly greater, that nearly two colored die for every white person out of equal numbers of each."

Morals and manners also suffered under the new dispensation. In the crowded and disease-stricken towns and camps, the conditions under which the roving negroes lived were no better for morals than for health, for here there were none of the

restraints to which the blacks had been accustomed and which they now despised as being a
part of their servitude. But in spite of all the
relief that could be given there was much want.
In fact, to restore former conditions the relief
agencies frequently cut off supplies in order to
force the negroes back to work and to prevent
others from leaving the country for the towns.
But the hungry freedmen turned to the nearest
food supply, and "spilin de gypshuns" (despoiling
the Egyptians, as the negroes called stealing from
the whites) became an approved means of support.
Thefts of hogs, cattle, poultry, field crops, and
vegetables drove almost to desperation those
whites who lived in the vicinity of the negro camps.
When the ex-slave felt obliged to go to town, he
was likely to take with him a team and wagon and
his master's clothes if he could get them.

The former good manners of the negro were
now replaced by impudence and distrust. There
were advisers among the negro troops and other
agitators who assured them that politeness to whites
was a mark of servitude. Pushing and crowding
in public places, on street cars and on the sidewalks,
and impudent speeches everywhere marked generally the limit of rudeness. And the negroes were,

in this respect, perhaps no worse than those European immigrants who act upon the principle that bad manners are a proof of independence.

The year following emancipation was one of religious excitement for large numbers of the blacks. Before 1865 the negro church members were attached to white congregations or were organized into missions, with nearly always a white minister in charge and a black assistant. With the coming of freedom the races very soon separated in religious matters. For this there were two principal reasons: the negro preachers could exercise more influence in independent churches; and new church organizations from the North were seeking negro membership. Sometimes negro members were urged to insist on the right "to sit together" with the whites. In a Richmond church a negro from the street pushed his way to the communion altar and knelt. There was a noticeable pause; then General Robert E. Lee went forward and knelt beside the negro; and the congregation followed his example. But this was a solitary instance. When the race issue was raised by either color, the church membership usually divided. There was much churchgoing by the negroes, day and night, and church festivities and baptisms were common. The blacks preferred immersion and wanted a new baptism each time they changed to a new church. Baptizings in ponds, creeks, or rivers were great occasions and were largely attended. "Shouting" the candidates went into the water and "shouting" they came out. One old woman came up screaming, "Freed from slavery! freed from sin! Bless God and General Grant!"

In the effort to realize their new-found freedom, the negroes were heavily handicapped by their extreme poverty and their ignorance. The total value of free negro property ran up into the millions in 1860, but the majority of the negroes had nothing. There were a few educated negroes in the South, and more in the North and in Canada, but the mass of the race was too densely ignorant to furnish its own leadership. The case, however, was not hopeless; the negro was able to work and in large territories had little competition; wages were high, even though paid in shares of the crop; the cost of living was low; and land was cheap. Thousands seemed thirsty for an education and crowded the schools which were available. It was too much, however, to expect the negro to take immediate advantage of his opportunities. What he wanted was a long holiday, a gun and a dog, and plenty of hunting and fishing. He must have Saturday at least for a trip to town or to a picnic or a circus; he did not wish to be a servant. When he had any money, swindlers reaped a harvest. They sold him worthless finery, cheap guns, preparations to bleach the skin or straighten the hair, and striped pegs which, when set up on the master's plantation, would entitle the purchaser to "40 acres and a mule."

The attitude of the negroes' employers not infrequently complicated the situation which they sought to better. The old masters were, as a rule, skeptical of the value of free negro labor. Carl Schurz thought this attitude boded ill for the future: "A belief, conviction, or prejudice, or whatever you may call it," he said, "so widely spread and apparently deeply rooted as this, that the negro will not work without physical compulsion, is certainly calculated to have a very serious influence upon the conduct of the people entertaining it. It naturally produced a desire to preserve slavery in its original form as much and as long as possible . . . or to introduce into the new system that element of physical compulsion which would make the negro work."

The negro wished to be free to leave his job when he pleased, but, as Benjamin C. Truman stated in his report to President Johnson, a "result of the settled belief in the negro's inferiority, and in the necessity that he should not be left to himself without a guardian, is that in some sections he is discouraged from leaving his old master. I have known of planters who considered it an offence against neighborhood courtesy for another to hire their old hands, and in two instances that were reported the disputants came to blows over the breach of etiquette." The new Freedmen's Bureau insisted upon written contracts, except for day laborers, and this undoubtedly kept many negroes from working regularly, for they were suspicious of contracts. Besides, the agitators and the negro troops led them to hope for an eventual distribution of property. An Alabama planter thus described the situation in December, 1865:

They will not work for anything but wages, and few are able to pay wages. They are penniless but resolute in their demands. They expect to see all the land divided out equally between them and their old masters in time to make the next crop. One of the most intelligent black men I know told me that in a neighboring village, where several hundred blacks were congregated, he does not think that as many as three made contracts, although planters are urgent in their solicitations and offering highest prices for labor they can possibly afford to pay. The same man informed me that the impression widely prevails that Congress is about to divide out the lands, and that this impression is given out by Federal soldiers at the nearest military station. It cannot be disguised that in spite of the most earnest efforts of their old master to conciliate and satisfy them, the estrangement between races increases in its extent and bitterness. Nearly all the negro men are armed with repeaters, and many of them carry them openly, day and night.

The relations between the races were better, however, than conditions seemed to indicate. The whites of the Black Belt were better disposed toward the negroes than were those of the white districts. It was in the towns and villages that most of the race conflicts occurred. All whites agreed that the negro was inferior, but there were many who were grateful for his conduct during the war and who wished him well. But others, the policemen of the towns, the "loyalists," those who had little but pride of race and the vote to distinguish them from the blacks, felt no good will toward the ex-slaves. It was Truman's opinion "not only that the planters are far better friends to the negroes than the poor whites, but also better than a majority of the Northern men who go South to rent plantations." John T. Trowbridge, the novelist, who recorded his impressions of the South after a visit in 1865, was of the opinion that the Unionists "do not like niggers." "For there is," he said, "more prejudice against color among the middle and poorer classes — the Union men of the South who owned few or no slaves — than among the planters who owned them by scores and hundreds." The reports of the Freedmen's Bureau are to the same effect. A Bureau agent in Tennessee testified: "An old citizen, a Union man, said to me, said he, 'I tell you what, if you take away the military from Tennessee, the buzzards can't eat up the niggers as fast as we'll kill them.'"

The lawlessness of the negroes in parts of the Black Belt and the disturbing influences of the black troops, of some officials of the Bureau, and of some of the missionary teachers and preachers, caused the whites to fear insurrections and to take measures for protection. Secret semi-military organizations were formed which later developed into the Ku Klux orders. When, however, New Year's Day, 1866, passed without the hoped-for distribution of property the negroes began to settle down.

At the beginning of the period of reconstruction it seemed possible that the negro race might speedily fall into distinct economic groups, for there were some who had property and many others who had the ability and the opportunity to acquire it; but the later drawing of race lines and the political disturbances of reconstruction checked this tendency. It was expected also that the Northern planters who came South in large numbers in 1865–66 might, by controlling the negro labor and by the use of more efficient methods, aid in the economic upbuilding of the country. But they were ignorant of agricultural matters and incapable of wisely controlling the blacks; and they failed because at one time they placed too much trust in the negroes and at another treated them too harshly and expected too much of them.

The question of negro suffrage was not a live issue in the South until the middle of 1866. There was almost no talk about it among the negroes; they did not know what it was. President Lincoln in 1864 and President Johnson in 1865 had merely mentioned the subject, though Chief Justice Chase and prominent radical members of Congress, as well as numerous abolitionists, had framed a negro suffrage platform. But the Southern whites, considering the matter an impossibility, gave it

4

little consideration. There was, however, both North and South, a tendency to see a connection between the freedom of the negroes and their political rights and thus to confuse civil equality with political and social privileges. But the great masses of the whites were solidly opposed to the recognition of negro equality in any form. The poorer whites, especially the "Unionists" who hoped to develop an opposition party, were angered by any discussion of the subject. An Alabama "Unionist," M. J. Saffold, later prominent as a radical politician, declared to the Joint Committee on Reconstruction: "If you compel us to carry through universal suffrage of colored men . . . it will prove quite an incubus upon us in the organization of a national union party of white men; it will furnish our opponents with a very effective weapon of offense against us."

There were, however, some Southern leaders of ability and standing who, by 1866, were willing to consider negro suffrage. These men, among them General Wade Hampton of South Carolina and Governor Robert Patton of Alabama, were of the slaveholding class, and they fully counted on being able to control the negro's vote by methods similar to those actually put in force a quarter of a

century later. The negroes were not as yet
politically organized, were not even interested in
politics, and the master class might reasonably
hope to regain control of them. Whitelaw Reid
published an interview with one of the Hamptons
which describes the situation exactly:

A brother of General Wade Hampton, the South
Carolina Hotspur, was on board. He saw no great
objection to negro suffrage, so far as the whites were
concerned; and for himself, South Carolinian and
secessionist though he was, he was quite willing to
accept it. He only dreaded its effect on the blacks
themselves. Hitherto they had in the main, been
modest and respectful, and mere freedom was not
likely to spoil them. But the deference to them likely
to be shown by partisans eager for their votes would
have a tendency to uplift them and unbalance them.
Beyond this, no harm would be done the South by negro
suffrage. The old owners would cast the votes of their
people almost as absolutely and securely as they cast
their own. If Northern men expected in this way to
build up a northern party in the South, they were
gravely mistaken. They would only be multiplying
the power of the old and natural leaders of Southern
politics by giving every vote to a former slave. Heretofore such men had served their masters only in the
fields; now they would do no less faithful service at the
polls. If the North could stand it, the South could.
For himself, he should make no special objection to
negro suffrage as one of the terms of reorganization, and

if it came, he did not think the South would have much cause to regret it.

To sum up the situation at this time: the negro population at the close of the war constituted a tremendous problem for those in authority. The race was free, but without status, without leaders, without property, and without education. Probably a fourth of them had some experience in freedom before the Confederate armies surrendered, and the servitude of the other three millions ended very quickly and without violence. But in the Black Belt, where the bulk of the black population was to be found, the labor system was broken up, and for several months the bewildered freedmen wandered about or remained at home under conditions which were bad for health, morals, and thrift. The Northern negroes did not furnish the expected leadership for the race, and the more capable men in the South showed a tendency to go North. The unsettled state of the negroes and their expectation of receiving a part of the property of the whites kept the latter uneasy and furnished the occasion of frequent conflicts. Not the least of the unsettling influences at work upon the negro population were the colored troops and the agitators furnished by the Freedmen's Bureau, the mis-

sions, and the Bureau schools.   But at the beginning of the year 1866 the situation appeared to be
clearing, and the social and economic revolution
seemed on the way to a quieter ending than might
have been expected.

CHAPTER III

THE WORK OF THE PRESIDENTS

THE war ended slavery, but it left the problem of the freed slave; it preserved the Union in theory, but it left unsolved many delicate problems of readjustment. Were the seceded States in or out of the Union? If in the Union, what rights had they? If they were not in the Union, what was their status? What was the status of the Southern Unionist, of the ex-Confederate? What punishments should be inflicted upon the Southern people? What authority, executive or legislative, should carry out the work of reconstruction? The end of the war brought with it, in spite of much discussion, no clear answer to these perplexing questions.

Unfortunately, American political life, with its controversies over colonial government, its conflicting interpretations of written constitutions, and its legally trained statesmen, had by the middle of the nineteenth century produced a habit of political thought which demanded the settlement of most governmental matters upon a theoretical basis. And now in 1865 each prominent leader had his own plan of reconstruction fundamentally irreconcilable with all the others, because rigidly theoretical. During the war the powers of the Executive had been greatly expanded and a legislative reaction was to be expected. The Constitution called for fresh interpretation in the light of the Civil War and its results.

The first theory of reconstruction may be found in the Crittenden-Johnson resolutions of July, 1861, which declared that the war was being waged to maintain the Union under the Constitution and that it should cease when these objects were obtained. This would have been subscribed to in 1861 by the Union Democrats and by most of the Republicans, and in 1865 the conquered Southerners would have been glad to reënter the Union upon this basis; but though in 1865 the resolution still expressed the views of many Democrats, the majority of Northern people had moved away from this position.

The attitude of Lincoln, which in 1865 met the views of a majority of the Northern people though not of the political leaders, was that "no State can upon its mere motion get out of the Union," that the States survived though there might be some doubt about state governments, and that "loyal" state organizations might be established by a population consisting largely of ex-Confederates who had been pardoned by the President and made "loyal" for the future by an oath of allegiance. Reconstruction was, Lincoln thought, a matter for the Executive to handle. But that he was not inflexibly committed to any one plan is indicated by his proclamation after the pocket veto of the Wade-Davis Bill and by his last speech, in which he declared that the question of whether the seceded States were in the Union or out of it was "merely a pernicious abstraction." In addition, Lincoln said:

We are all agreed that the seceded States, so called, are out of their proper practical relation with the Union, and that the sole object of the government, civil and military, in regard to those States is to again get them into that proper practical relation. I believe that it is not only possible, but in fact easier, to do this without deciding or even considering whether these States have ever been out of the Union, than with it. Finding themselves safely at home, it would be utterly immaterial whether they had ever been abroad. Let us all join in doing the acts necessary to restore the proper practical relations between these States and the Union, and each forever after innocently indulge his own opinion whether in doing the acts he brought the States from without into the Union, or only gave them proper assistance, they never having been out of it.

President Johnson's position was essentially that of Lincoln, but his attitude toward the working out of the several problems was different. He maintained that the States survived and that it was the duty of the Executive to restore them to their proper relations. "The true theory," said he, "is that all pretended acts of secession were from the beginning null and void. The States cannot commit treason nor screen individual citizens who may have committed treason any more than they can make valid treaties or engage in lawful commerce with any foreign power. The States attempting to secede placed themselves in a condition where their vitality was impaired, but not extinguished; their functions suspended, but not destroyed." Lincoln would have had no severe punishments inflicted even on leaders, but Johnson wanted to destroy the "slavocracy," root and branch. Confiscation of estates would, he thought, be a proper measure. He said on one occasion: "Traitors should take a back seat in the work of restoration. . . . My judgment is that he [a rebel] should be subjected to a severe ordeal before he is restored to citizenship. Treason should be made odious, and traitors must be punished and impoverished. Their great plantations must be seized, and divided into small farms and sold to honest, industrious men." The violence of Johnson's views subsequently underwent considerable modification but to the last he held to the plan of executive restoration based upon state perdurance. Neither Lincoln nor Johnson favored a change of Southern institutions other than the abolition of slavery, though each recommended a qualified negro suffrage.

There were, however, other theories in the field, notably those of the radical Republican leaders. According to the state-suicide theory of Charles Sumner, "any vote of secession or other act by which any State may undertake to put an end to the supremacy of the Constitution within its territory is inoperative and void against the Constitution, and when sustained by force it becomes a practical *abdication* by the State of all rights under the Constitution, while the treason it involves still further works an instant *forfeiture* of all those functions and powers essential to the continued existence of the State as a body politic, so that from that time forward the territory falls under the exclusive jurisdiction of Congress as other territory, and the State, being according to the language of the law *felo de se*, ceases to exist." Congress should punish the "rebels" by abolishing slavery, by giving civil and political rights to negroes, and by educating them with the whites.

Not essentially different, but harsher, was Thaddeus Stevens's plans for treating the South as a conquered foreign province. Let the victors treat the seceded States "as conquered provinces and settle them with new men and exterminate or drive out the present rebels as exiles." Congress in dealing with these provinces was not bound even by the Constitution, "a bit of worthless parchment," but might legislate as it pleased in regard to slavery, the ballot, and confiscation. With regard to the white population he said: "I have never desired bloody punishments to any great extent. But there are punishments quite as appalling, and longer remembered, than death. They are more advisable, because they would reach a greater number. Strip a proud nobility of their bloated estates; reduce them to a level with plain republicans; send them forth to labor, and teach their children to enter the workshops or handle a plow,

and you will thus humble the proud traitors."
Stevens and Sumner agreed in reducing the Southern States to a territorial status. Sumner would then take the principles of the Declaration of Independence as a guide for Congress, while Stevens would leave Congress absolute. Neither considered the Constitution as of any validity in this crisis.

As a rule the former abolitionists were in 1865 advocates of votes and lands for the negro, in whose capacity for self-rule they had complete confidence. The view of Gerrit Smith may be regarded as typical of the abolitionist position:

Let the first condition of peace with them be that no people in the rebel States shall ever lose or gain civil or political rights by reason of their race or origin. The next condition of peace be that our black allies in the South — those saviours of our nation — shall share with their poor white neighbors in the subdivisions of the large landed estates of the South. Let the only other condition be that the rebel masses shall not, for say, a dozen years, be allowed access to the ballot-box, or be eligible to office; and that the like restrictions be for life on their political and military leaders. . . . The mass of the Southern blacks fall, in point of intelligence, but little, if any, behind the mass of the Southern whites. . . . In reference to the qualifications of the voter, men make too much account of the head and too little of the heart. The ballot-box, like God, says: "Give me your heart."

The best-hearted men are the best qualified to vote; and, in this light, the blacks, with their characteristic gentleness, patience, and affectionateness, are peculiarly entitled to vote. We cannot wonder at Swedenborg's belief that the celestial people will be found in the interior of Africa; nor hardly can we wonder at the legend that the gods came down every year to sup with their favorite Africans.

One of the most statesmanlike proposals was made by Governor John A. Andrew of Massachusetts. If, forgetting their theories, the conservatives could have united in support of a restoration conceived in his spirit, the goal might have been speedily achieved. Andrew demanded a reorganization, based upon acceptance of the results of the war, but carried through with the aid of "those who are by their intelligence and character the natural leaders of their people and who surely will lead them by and by." These men cannot be kept out forever, said he, for

the capacity of leadership is a gift, not a device. They whose courage, talents, and will entitle them to lead, will lead. . . . If we cannot gain their support of the just measures needful for the work of safe reorganization, reorganization will be delusive and full of danger. They are the most hopeful subjects to deal with. They have the brain and the experience and the education to enable them to understand . . . the present situation.

They have the courage as well as the skill to lead the people in the direction their judgments point. . . . Is it consistent with reason and our knowledge of human nature, to believe the masses of Southern men able to face about, to turn their backs on those they have trusted and followed, and to adopt the lead of those who have no magnetic hold on their hearts or minds? It would be idle to reorganize by the colored vote. If the popular vote of the white race is not to be had in favor of the guarantees justly required, then I am in favor of holding on — just where we are now. I am not in favor of a surrender of the present rights of the Union to a struggle between a white minority aided by the freedmen on one hand, against the majority of the white race on the other. I would not consent, having rescued those states by arms from Secession and rebellion, to turn them over to anarchy and chaos.

The Southerners, Unionists as well as Confederates, had their views as well, but at Washington these carried little influence. The former Confederates would naturally favor the plan which promised best for the white South, and their views were most nearly met by those of President Lincoln. Although he held that in principle a new Union had arisen out of the war, as a matter of immediate political expediency he was prepared to build on the assumption that the old Union still existed. The Southern Unionists cared little for theories; they wanted the Confederates punished, themselves promoted to high offices, and the negro kept from the ballot box.

Even at the beginning of 1866, it was not too much to hope that the majority of former Republicans would accept conservative methods, provided the so-called "fruits of the war" were assured — that is, equality of civil rights, the guarantee of the United States war debt, the repudiation of the Confederate debt, the temporary disfranchisement of the leading Confederates, and some arrangement which would keep the South from profiting by representation based on the non-voting negro population. But amid many conflicting policies, none attained to continuous and compelling authority.

The plan first put to trial was that of President Lincoln. It was a definite plan designed to meet actual conditions and, had he lived, he might have been able to carry it through successfully. Not a theorist, but an opportunist of the highest type, sobered by years of responsibility in war time, and fully understanding the precarious situation in 1865, Lincoln was most anxious to secure an early restoration of solidarity with as little friction as possible. Better than most Union leaders he appreciated conditions in the South, the problem of the races, the weakness of the Southern Unionists, and the advantage of calling in the old Southern leaders. He was generous and considerate; he wanted no executions or imprisonments; he wished the leaders to escape; and he was anxious that the mass of Southerners be welcomed back without loss of rights. "There is," he declared, "too little respect for their rights," an unwillingness, in short, to treat them as fellow citizens.

This executive policy had been applied from the beginning of the war as opportunity offered. The President used the army to hold the Border States in the Union, to aid in "reorganizing" Unionist Virginia and in establishing West Virginia. The army, used to preserve the Union might be used also to restore disturbed parts of it to normal condition. Assuming that the "States" still existed, "loyal" state governments were the first necessity. By his proclamation of December 8, 1863, Lincoln suggested a method of beginning the reconstruction: he would pardon any Confederate, except specified classes of leaders, who took an oath of loyalty for the future; if as many as ten per cent of the voting population of 1860, thus made loyal, should establish a state government the Executive would recognize it. The matter of slavery must, indeed, be left to the laws and proclamations as interpreted by the courts, but other institutions should continue as in 1861.

This plan was inaugurated in four States which had been in part controlled by the Federal army from nearly the beginning of the war: Tennessee (1862), Louisiana (1862), Arkansas (1862), and Virginia after the formation of West Virginia (1863). For each State, Lincoln appointed a military governor: for Tennessee, Andrew Johnson; for Arkansas, John S. Phelps; for Louisiana, General Shepley. In Virginia he recognized the "reorganized" government, which had been transferred to Alexandria when the new State of West Virginia was formed. The military governors undertook the slow and difficult work of reorganization, however, with but slight success owing to the small numbers of Unionists and of Confederates who would take the oath. But by 1864 "ten per cent" state governments were established in Arkansas and Louisiana, and progress was being made in Tennessee.

Congress was impatient of Lincoln's claim to executive precedence in the matter of reconstruction, and in 1864 both Houses passed the Wade-Davis Bill, a plan which asserted the right of Congress to control reconstruction and foreshadowed a

5

radical settlement of the question. Lincoln disposed of the bill by a pocket veto and, in a proclamation dated July 8, 1864, stated that he was unprepared "to be inflexibly committed to any single plan of restoration," or to discourage loyal citizens by setting aside the governments already established in Louisiana and Arkansas, or to recognize the authority of Congress to abolish slavery. He was ready, however, to coöperate with the people of any State who wished to accept the plan prepared by Congress and he hoped that a constitutional amendment abolishing slavery would be adopted.

Lincoln early came to the conclusion that slavery must be destroyed, and he had urgently advocated deportation of the freedmen, for he believed that the two races could not live in harmony after emancipation. The nearest he came to recommending the vote for the negro was in a communication to Governor Hahn of Louisiana in March, 1864: "I barely suggest, for your private consideration, whether some of the colored people may not be let in, as for instance, the very intelligent, and especially those who have fought gallantly in our ranks. They would probably help, in some trying time to come, to keep the jewel of liberty within the family of freedom. But this is only a suggestion, not to the public, but to you alone."

Throughout the war President Lincoln assumed that the state organizations in the South were illegal because disloyal and that new governments must be established. But just at the close of the war, probably carried away by feeling, he all but recognized the Virginia Confederate Government as competent to bring the State back into the Union. While in Richmond on April 5, 1865, he gave to Judge Campbell a statement of terms: the national authority to be restored; no recession on slavery by the Executive; hostile forces to disband. The next day he notified General Weitzel, in command at Richmond, that he might permit the Virginia Legislature to meet and withdraw military and other support from the Confederacy. But these measures met strong opposition in Washington, especially from Secretary Stanton and Senator Wade and other congressional leaders, and on the 11th of April Lincoln withdrew his permission for the Legislature to meet. "I cannot go forward," he said, "with everybody opposed to me." It was on the same day that he made his last public speech, and Sumner, who was strongly opposed to his policy, remarked that "the President's

speech and other things augur confusion and uncertainty in the future, with hot contumacy." At
a cabinet meeting on the 14th of April, Lincoln
made his last statement on the subject. It was
fortunate, he said, that Congress had adjourned,
for "we shall reanimate the States" before Congress meets; there should be no killing, no persecu-
tions; there was too much disposition to treat the
Southern people "not as fellow citizens."

The possibility of a conciliatory restoration
ended when Lincoln was assassinated. Moderate,
firm, tactful, of great personal influence, not a
doctrinaire, and not a Southerner like Johnson,
Lincoln might have "prosecuted peace" successfully. His policy was very unlike that proposed
by the radical leaders. They would base the new
governments upon the loyalty of the past plus the
aid of enfranchised slaves; he would establish the
new régime upon the loyalty of the future. Like
Governor Andrew he thought that restoration must
be effected by the willing efforts of the South. He
would aid and guide but not force the people. If
the latter did not wish restoration, they might
remain under military rule. There should be no
forced negro suffrage, no sweeping disfranchisement of whites, no "carpetbaggism."

ANDREW JOHNSON

Engraving after a photograph by Brady.

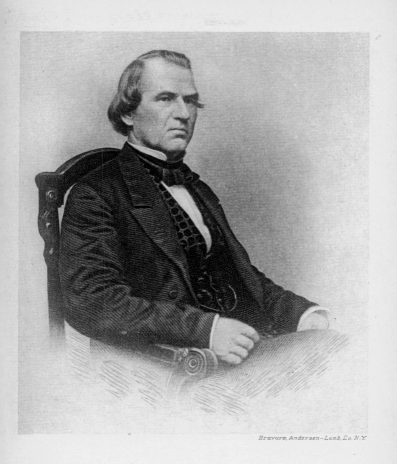

Bravure, Andersen-Lamb, Co. N.Y.

The work of President Johnson demands for its proper understanding some consideration of the condition of the political parties at the close of the war, for politics had much to do with reconstruction. The Democratic party, divided and defeated in the election of 1860, lost its Southern members in 1861 by the secession and remained a minority party during the remainder of the war. It retained its organization, however, and in 1864 polled a large vote. Discredited by its policy of opposition to Lincoln's Administration, its ablest leaders joined the Republicans in support of the war. Until 1869 the party was poorly represented in Congress although, as soon as hostilities ended, the War Democrats showed a tendency to return to the old party. As to reconstruction, the party stood on the Crittenden-Johnson resolutions of 1861, though most Democrats were now willing to have slavery abolished.

The Republican party — frankly sectional and going into power on the single issue of opposition to the extension of slavery — was forced by the secession movement to take up the task of preserving the Union by war. Consequently, the party developed new principles, welcomed the aid of the War Democrats, and found it advisable to drop its name and with its allies to form the Union or National Union party. It was this National Union party which in 1864 nominated Abraham Lincoln, a Republican, and Andrew Johnson, a Democrat, on the same ticket. Lincoln's second Cabinet was composed of both Republicans and War Democrats. When the war ended, the conservative leaders were anxious to hold the Union party together in order to be in a better position to settle the problems of reconstruction, but the movement of the War Democrats back to their old party tended to leave in the Union party only its Republican members, with the radical leaders dominating.

In the South the pressure of war so united the people that party divisions disappeared for a time, but the causes of division continued to exist and two parties, at least, would have developed had the pressure been removed. Though all factions supported the war after it began, the former Whigs and Douglas Democrats, when it was over, liked to remember that they had been "Union" men in 1860 and expected to organize in opposition to the extreme Democrats, who were now charged with being responsible for the misfortunes of the South. They were in a position to affiliate with the

National Union party of the North if proper in-
ducements were offered, while the regular Democrats were ready to rejoin their old party. But the
embittered feelings resulting from the murder of
Lincoln and the rapid development of the struggle
between President Johnson and Congress caused
the radicals "to lump the old Union Democrats
and Whigs together with the secessionists — and
many were driven where they did not want to
go, into temporary affiliation with the Democratic
party." Thousands went very reluctantly; the
old Whigs, indeed, were not firmly committed to
the Democrats until radical reconstruction had actually begun. Still other "loyalists" in the South
were prepared to join the Northern radicals in advocating the disfranchisement of Confederates and in
opposing the granting of suffrage to the negroes.

The man upon whom fell the task of leading
these opposing factions, radical and conservative,
along a definite line of action looking to reunion
had few qualifications for the task. Johnson was
ill-educated, narrow, and vindictive and was posi-
tive that those who did not agree with him were
dishonest. Himself a Southerner, picked up by the
National Union Convention of 1864, as Thaddeus
Stevens said, from "one of those damned rebel

provinces," he loved the Union, worshiped the Constitution, and held to the strict construction views of the State Rights Democrats. Rising from humble beginnings, he was animated by the most intense dislike of the "slavocracy," as he called the political aristocracy of the South. Like many other American leaders he was proud of his humble origin, but unlike many others he never sloughed off his backwoods crudeness. He continually boasted of himself and vilified the aristocrats, who in return treated him badly. His dislike of them was so marked that Isham G. Harris, a rival politician, remarked that "if Johnson were a snake, he would lie in the grass to bite the heels of rich men's children." His primitive notions of punishment were evident in 1865 when he advocated imprisonment, execution, and confiscation; but like other reckless talkers he often said more than he meant.

When Johnson succeeded to the presidency, the feeling was nearly universal among the radicals, according to Julian, that he would prove a godsend to the country, for "aside from Mr. Lincoln's known policy of tenderness to the rebels, which now so jarred upon the feelings of the hour, his well known views on the subject of reconstruction were as distasteful as possible to radical Republicans."

Senator Wade declared to the President: "Johnson, we have faith in you. By the gods, there will be no trouble now in running the Government!" To which Johnson replied: "Treason is a crime and crime must be punished. Treason must be made infamous and traitors must be impoverished." These words are an index to the speeches of Johnson during 1863–65. Even his radical friends feared that he would be too vindictive. For a few weeks he was much inclined to the radical plans, and some of the leaders certainly understood that he was in favor of negro suffrage, the supreme test of radicalism. But when the excitement caused by the assassination of Lincoln and the break-up of the Confederacy had moderated somewhat, Johnson saw before him a task so great that his desire for violent measures was chilled. He must disband the great armies and bring all war work to an end; he must restore intercourse with the South, which had been blockaded for years; he must for a time police the country, look after the negroes, and set up a temporary civil government; and finally he must work out a restoration of the Union. Sobered by responsibility and by the influence of moderate advisers, he rather quickly adopted Lincoln's policy.

Johnson at first set his face against the movements toward reconstruction by the state governments already organized and by those people who wished to organize new governments on Lincoln's ten per cent plan. As soon as possible the War Department notified the Union commanders to stop all attempts at reconstruction and to pursue and arrest all Confederate governors and other prominent civil leaders. The President was even anxious to arrest the military leaders who had been paroled but was checked in this desire by General Grant's firm protest. His cabinet advisers supported Johnson in refusing to recognize the Southern state governments; but three of them — Seward, Welles, and McCulloch — were influential in moderating his zeal for inflicting punishments. Nevertheless he soon had in prison the most prominent of the Confederate civilians and several general officers. The soldiers, however, were sent home, trade with the South was permitted, and the Freedmen's Bureau was rapidly extended.

Previous to this Johnson had brought himself to recognize, early in May, the Lincoln "ten per cent" governments of Louisiana, Tennessee, and Arkansas, and the reconstructed Alexandria government of Virginia. Thus only seven States were left without legal governments, and to bring those States back into the Union Johnson inaugurated on May 29, 1865, a plan which was like that of Lincoln but not quite so liberal. In his Amnesty Proclamation, Johnson made a longer list of exceptions aimed especially at the once wealthy slave owners. On the same day he proclaimed the restoration of North Carolina. A provisional governor, W. W. Holden, was appointed and directed to reorganize the civil government and to call a constitutional convention elected by those who had taken the amnesty oath. This convention was to make necessary amendments to the constitution and to "restore said State to its constitutional relations to the Federal Government." It is to be noted that Johnson fixed the qualifications of delegates and of those who elected them, but, this stage once passed, the convention or the legislature would "prescribe the qualifications of electors . . . a power the people of the several States composing the Federal Union have rightfully exercised from the origin of the government to the present time." The President also directed the various cabinet officers to extend the work of their departments over the Confederate States and ordered the army officers to assist the civil authorities. During the next six weeks similar measures were undertaken for the remaining six States of the Confederacy.

To set up the new order army officers were first sent into every county to administer the amnesty oath and thus to secure a "loyal" electorate. In each State the provisional governor organized out of the remains of the Confederate local régime a new civil government. Confederate local officials who could and would take the amnesty oath were directed to resume office until relieved; the laws of 1861, except those relating to slavery, were declared to be in force; the courts were directed to use special efforts to crush lawlessness; and the old jury lists were destroyed and new ones were drawn up containing only the names of those who had taken the amnesty oath. Since there was no money in any state treasury, small sums were now raised by license taxes. A full staff of department heads was appointed, and by July, 1865, the provisional governments were in fair working order.

To the constitutional conventions, which met in the fall, it was made clear, through the governors, that the President would insist upon three conditions: the formal abolition of slavery, the repudiation of the ordinance of secession, and the repudiation of the Confederate war debt. To Governor Holden he telegraphed: "Every dollar of the debt created to aid the rebellion against the United States should be repudiated finally and for-ever. The great mass of the people should not be taxed to pay a debt to aid in carrying on a rebellion which they in fact, if left to themselves, were op-posed to. Let those who had given their means for the obligations of the state look to that power they tried to establish in violation of law, constitution, and will of the people. They must meet their fate." With little opposition these conditions were fulfilled, though there was a strong feeling against the repudiation of the debt, much discussion as to whether the ordinance of secession should be "re-pealed" or declared "now and always null and void," and some quibbling as to whether slavery was being destroyed by state action or had already been destroyed by war.

In the old state constitutions, very slight changes were made. Of these the chief were concerned with the abolition of slavery and the arrangement of representation and direct taxation on the basis of white population. Little effort was made to settle any of the negro problems, and in all States the conventions left it to the legislatures to make laws for the freedmen. There was no discussion of negro suffrage in the conventions, but President Johnson sent what was for him a remarkable communication to Governor Sharkey of Mississippi:

If you could extend the elective franchise to all persons of color who can read the Constitution of the United States in English and write their names, and to all persons of color who own real estate valued at not less than two hundred and fifty dollars and pay taxes thereon, you would completely disarm the adversary and set an example the other States will follow. This you can do with perfect safety, and you would thus place Southern States in reference to free persons of color upon the same basis with the free States. . . . And as a consequence the radicals, who are wild upon negro franchise, will be completely foiled in their attempts to keep the Southern States from renewing their relations to the Union by not accepting their senators and representatives.

In deciding upon a basis of representation it was clear that the majority of delegates desired to lessen the influence of the Black Belt and place the control of the government with the "up country." In the Alabama convention Robert M. Patton, then a delegate and later governor, frankly avowed this object, and in South Carolina Governor Perry urged the convention to give no consideration to negro suffrage, "because this is a white man's government," and if the negroes should vote they would be controlled by a few whites. A kindly disposition toward the negroes was general except on the part of extreme Unionists, who opposed any favors to the race. "This is a white man's country" was a doctrine to which all the conventions subscribed.

The conventions held brief sessions, completed their work, and adjourned, after directing that elections be held for state and local officers and for members of Congress. Before December the appointed local officials had been succeeded by elected officers; members of Congress were on their way to Washington; the state legislatures were assembling or already in session; and the elected governors were ready to take office. It was understood that as soon as enough state legislatures ratified the Thirteenth Amendment to make it a part of the Constitution, the President would permit the transfer of authority to the new governors. The Legislature of Mississippi alone was recalcitrant about the amendment, and before January, 1866, the elected officials were everywhere installed except in Texas, where the work was not completed until March. When Congress met in December, 1865, the President reported that all former Confederate States except Texas were

ready to be readmitted. Congress, however, refused to admit their senators and representatives,
and thus began the struggle which ended over a
year later with the victory of the radicals and the
undoing of the work of the two Presidents.

The plan of the Presidents was at best only im-
perfectly realized. It was found impossible to reorganize the Federal Administration in the South
with men who could subscribe to the "ironclad
oath," for nearly all who were competent to hold
office had favored or aided the Confederacy. It
was two years before more than a third of the
post offices could be opened. The other Federal
departments were in similar difficulties, and at
last women and "carpetbaggers" were appointed.
The Freedmen's Bureau, which had been established coincidently with the provisional governments, assumed jurisdiction over the negroes, while
the army authorities very early took the position that any man who claimed to be a Unionist
should not be tried in the local courts but must be
given a better chance in a provost court. Thus a
third or more of the population was withdrawn
from the control of the state government. In several States the head of the Bureau made arrangements for local magistrates and officials to act as

Bureau officials, and in such cases the two authorities acted in coöperation. The army of occupation, too, exerted an authority which not infrequently interfered with the workings of the new state government. Nearly everywhere there was a lack of certainty and efficiency due to the concurrent and sometimes conflicting jurisdictions of state government, army commanders, Bureau authorities, and even the President acting upon or through any of the others.

The standing of the Southern state organizations was in doubt after the refusal of Congress to recognize them. Nevertheless, in spite of this uncertainty they continued to function as States during the year of controversy which followed; the courts were opened and steadily grew in influence; here and there militia and patrols were reorganized; officials who refused to "accept the situation" were dismissed; elections were held; the legislatures revised the laws to fit new conditions and enacted new laws for the emancipated blacks. To all this progress in reorganization the action of Congress was a severe blow, since it gave notice that none of the problems of reconstruction were yet solved. An increasing spirit of irritation and independence was observed throughout the States in question,

6

and at the elections the former Confederates gained more and more offices. The year was marked in the South by the tendency toward the formation of parties, by the development of the "Southern outrages" issue, by an attempt to frustrate radical action, and finally by a line-up of the great mass of the whites in opposition to the Fourteenth Amendment and other radical plans of Congress.

The Joint Committee on Reconstruction, appointed when Congress refused to accept the work of President Johnson, proceeded during several months to take testimony and to consider measures. The testimony, which was taken chiefly to support opinions already formed, appeared to prove that the negroes and the Unionists were so badly treated that the Freedmen's Bureau and the army must be kept in the South to protect them; that free negro labor was a success but that the whites were hostile to it; that the whites were disloyal and would, if given control of the Southern governments and admitted to Congress, constitute a danger to the nation and especially to the party in power.

To convince the voters of the North of the necessity of dealing drastically with the South a campaign of misrepresentation was begun in the

summer of 1865, which became more and more
systematic and unscrupulous as the political struggle at Washington grew fiercer. Newspapers regularly ran columns headed "Southern Outrages"
and every conceivable mistreatment of blacks
by whites was represented as taking place on a
large scale. As General Richard Taylor said,
it would seem that about 1866 every white man,
woman, and child in the South began killing and
maltreating negroes. In truth, there was less and
less ground for objection to the treatment of the
blacks as time went on and as the several agencies
of government secured firmer control over the
lawless elements. But fortunately for the radicals
their contention seemed to be established by riots
on a large scale in Memphis and New Orleans
where negroes were killed and injured in much
greater number than whites.

The rapid development of the radical plans of
Congress checked the tendency toward political
division in the South. Only a small party of rabid
Unionists would now affiliate with the radicals,
while all the others reluctantly held together, endorsed Johnson's policy, and attempted to affiliate with the disintegrating National Union party.
But the defeat of the President's policies in the

elections of 1866, the increasing radicalism of Congress as shown by the Civil Rights Act, the expansion of the Freedmen's Bureau, the report of the Joint Committee on Reconstruction, and the proposal of the Fourteenth Amendment led far-sighted Southerners to see that the President was likely to lose in his fight with Congress.

Now began, in the latter half of 1866, with some coöperation in the North and probably with the approval of the President, a movement in the South to forestall the radicals by means of a settlement which, although less severe than the proposed Fourteenth Amendment, might yet be acceptable to Congress. One feature of the settlement was to be some form of negro suffrage, either by local action or by constitutional amendment. Those behind this scheme were mainly of the former governing class. Negro suffrage, they thought, would take the wind out of the radical sails, the Southern whites would soon be able to control the blacks, representation in Congress would be increased, and the Black Belt would perhaps regain its former political hegemony. It is hardly necessary to say that the majority of the whites were solidly opposed to such a measure. But it was hoped to carry it under pressure through the

Legislature or to bring it about indirectly through rulings of the Freedmen's Bureau.

Coincident with this scheme of partial negro suffrage an attempt was made by the conservative leaders in Washington, working with the Southerners, to propose a revised Fourteenth Amendment which would give the vote to competent negroes and not disfranchise the whites. A conference of Southern governors met in Washington early in 1867 and drafted such an amendment. But it was too late.

Meanwhile the Fourteenth Amendment submitted by Congress had been brought before the Southern legislatures and during the winter of 1866–67 it was rejected by all of them. There was strong opposition to it because it disfranchised the leading whites, but perhaps the principal reason for its rejection was that the Southern people were not sure that still more severe conditions might not be imposed later.

While the President was "restoring" the States which had seceded and struggling with Congress, the Border States of the South, including Tennessee (which was admitted in 1866 by reason of its radical state government), were also in the throes of reconstruction. Though there was less military interference in these than in the other States, many of the problems were similar. All had the Freedmen's Bureau, the negro race, the Unionists, and the Confederates; in every State, except Kentucky, Confederates were persecuted, the minority was in control, and "ring" rule was the order of the day; but in each State there were signs of the political revolution which a few years later was to put the radicals out of power.

The executive plan for the restoration of the Union, begun by Lincoln and adopted by Johnson, was, as we have seen, at first applied in all the States which had seceded. A military governor was appointed in each State by the President by virtue of his authority as commander in chief. This official, aided by a civilian staff of his own choice and supported by the United States army and other Federal agencies, reorganized the state administration and after a few months turned the state and local governments over to regularly elected officials. Restoration should now have been completed, but Congress refused to admit the senators and representatives of these States, and entered upon a fifteen months' struggle with the President over details of the methods of the reconstruction. Meanwhile the Southern States, though unrepresented in

Congress, continued their activities, with some interference from Federal authorities, until Congress in 1867 declared their governments non-existent.

The work begun by Lincoln and Johnson deserved better success. The original plan restored to political rights only a small number of Unionists, the lukewarm Confederates, and the unimportant. But in spite of the threatening speeches of Johnson he used his power of pardon until none except the most prominent leaders were excluded. The personnel of the Johnson governments was fair. The officials were, in the main, former Douglas Democrats and Whigs, respectable and conservative, but not admired or loved by the people. The conventions and the legislatures were orderly and dignified and manifested a desire to accept the situation.

There were no political parties at first, but material for several existed. If things had been allowed to take their course there would have arisen a normal cleavage between former Whigs and Democrats, between the up-country and the low country, between the slaveholders and the non-slaveholders. The average white man in these governments was willing to be fair to the negro but was not greatly concerned about his future. In the view of most white people it was the white man who was emancipated. The white districts had no desire to let the power return to the Black Belt by giving the negro the ballot, for the vote of the negroes, they believed, would be controlled by their former masters.

Johnson's adoption of Lincoln's plan gave notice to all that the radicals had failed to control him. He and they had little in common; they wished to uproot a civilization, while he wished to punish individuals; they were not troubled by constitutional scruples, while he was the strictest of State Rights Democrats; they thought principally of the negro and his potentialities, while Johnson was thinking of the emancipated white man. It is possible that Lincoln might have succeeded, but for Johnson the task proved too great.

CHAPTER IV

THE WARDS OF THE NATION

THE negroes at the close of the war were not slaves
or serfs, nor were they citizens. What was to be
done with them and for them? The Southern
answer to this question may be found in the so-
called "Black Laws," which were enacted by the
state governments set up by President Johnson.
The views of the dominant North may be dis-
cerned in part in the organization and administration of the Freedmen's Bureau. The two sections
saw the same problem from different angles and
their proposed solutions were of necessity opposed
in principle and in practice.

The South desired to fit the emancipated negro
race into the new social order by frankly recogniz-
ing his inferiority to the whites. In some things
racial separation was unavoidable. New legislation consequently must be enacted, because the
slave codes were obsolete; because the old laws

made for the small free negro class did not meet present conditions; and because the emancipated blacks could not be brought conveniently and at once under laws originally devised for a white population. The new laws must meet many needs; family life, morals, and conduct must be regulated; the former slave must be given a status in court in order that he might be protected in person and property; the old, the infirm, and the orphans must be cared for; the white race must be protected from lawless blacks and the blacks from unscrupulous and violent whites; the negro must have an opportunity for education; and the roving blacks must be forced to get homes, settle down, and go to work.

Pending such legislation the affairs of the negro remained in control of the unpopular Freedmen's Bureau — a "system of espionage," as Judge Clayton of Alabama called it, and, according to Governor Humphreys of Mississippi, "a hideous curse" under which white men were persecuted and pillaged. Judge Memminger of South Carolina, in a letter to President Johnson, emphasized the fact that the whites of England and the United States gained civil and political rights through centuries of slow advancement and that they were far ahead of the people of European states. Consequently, it would be a mistake to give the freedmen a status equal to that of the most advanced whites. Rather, let the United States profit by the experience of the British in their emancipation policies and arrange a system of apprenticeship for a period of transition. When the negro should be fit, let him be advanced to citizenship.

Most Southern leaders agreed that the removal of the master's protection was a real loss to the negro which must be made good to some extent by giving the negro a status in court and by accepting negro testimony in all cases in which blacks were concerned. The North Carolina committee on laws for freedmen agreed with objectors that "there are comparatively few of the slaves lately freed who are honest" and truthful, but maintained that the negroes were capable of improvement. The chief executives of Mississippi and Florida declared that there was no danger to the whites in admitting the more or less unreliable negro testimony, for the courts and juries would in every case arrive at a proper valuation of it. Governors Marvin of Florida and Humphreys of Mississippi advocated practical civil equality, while in North Carolina and several other States there was a disposition to admit negro testimony only in cases in which negroes were concerned. The North Carolina committee recommended the abolition of whipping as a punishment unfit for free people, and most States accepted this principle. Even in 1865 the general disposition was to make uniform laws for both races, except in regard to violation of contracts, immoral conduct, vagrancy, marriage, schools, and forms of punishment. In some of these matters the whites were to be more strictly regulated; in others, the negroes.

There was further general agreement that in economic relations both races must be protected, each from the other; but it is plain that the leaders believed that the negro had less at stake than the white. The negro was disposed to be indolent; he knew little of the obligations of contracts; he was not honest; and he would leave his job at will. Consequently Memminger recommended apprenticeship for all negroes; Governor Marvin suggested it for children alone; and others wished it provided for orphans only. Further, the laws enacted must force the negroes to settle down, to work, and to hold to contracts. Memminger showed that, without legislation to enforce contracts and to secure eviction of those who refused to work, the white planter in the South was wholly at the mercy of the negro. The plantations were scattered, the laborers' houses were already occupied, and there was no labor market to which a planter could go if the laborers deserted his fields.

What would the negro become if these leaders of reconstruction were to have their way? Something better than a serf, something less than a citizen — a second degree citizen, perhaps, with legal rights about equal to those of white women and children. Governor Marvin hoped to make of the race a good agricultural peasantry; his successor was anxious that the blacks should be preferred to European immigrants; others agreed with Memminger that after training and education he might be advanced to full citizenship.

These opinions are representative of those held by the men who, Memminger excepted, were placed in charge of affairs by President Johnson and who were not specially in sympathy with the negroes or with the planters but rather with the average white. All believed that emancipation was a mistake, but all agreed that "it is not the negro's fault" and gave no evidence of a disposition to perpetuate slavery under another name.

The legislation finally framed showed in its

discriminatory features the combined influence of the old laws for free negroes, the vagrancy laws of North and South for whites, the customs of slavery times, the British West Indies legislation for ex-slaves, and the regulations of the United States War and Treasury Departments and of the Freedmen's Bureau — all modified and elaborated by the Southern whites. In only two States, Mississippi and South Carolina, did the legislation bulk large in quantity; in other States discriminating laws were few; in still other States none were passed except those defining race and prohibiting intermarriage.

In all of the state laws there were certain common characteristics, among which were the following: the descendant of a negro was to be classed as a negro through the third generation,[1] even though one parent in each generation was white; intermarriage of the races was prohibited; existing slave marriages were declared valid and for the future marriage was generally made easier for the blacks than for the whites. In all States the negro was given his day in court, and in cases relating to negroes his testimony was accepted; in six States he might testify in any case. When provision was

[1] Fourth in Tennessee.

made for schooling, the rule of race separation was enforced. In Mississippi the "Jim Crow car," or separate car for negroes, was invented. In several States the negro had to have a license to carry weapons, to preach, or to engage in trade. In Mississippi, a negro could own land only in town; in other States he could purchase land only in the country. Why the difference, no one knows and probably few knew at the time. Some of the legislation was undoubtedly hasty and ill-considered.

But the laws relating to apprenticeship, vagrancy, and enforced punitive employment turned out to be of greater practical importance. On these subjects the legislation of Mississippi and South Carolina was the most extreme. In Mississippi negro orphans were to be bound out, preferably to a former master, if "he or she shall be a suitable person." The master was given the usual control over apprentices and was bound by the usual duties, including that of teaching the apprentice. But the penalties for "enticing away" apprentices were severe. The South Carolina statute was not essentially different. The vagrancy laws of these two States were in the main the same for both races, but in Mississippi the definition of vagrancy was enlarged to include negroes not at work, those "found unlawfully assembling themselves together," and "all white persons assembling themselves with freedmen." It is to be noted that nearly all punishment for petty offenses took the form of hiring out, preferably to the former master or employer. The principal petty offenses were, it would seem, vagrancy and "enticing away" laborers or apprentices. The South Carolina statute contains some other interesting provisions. A negro, man or woman, who had enjoyed the companionship of two or more spouses, must by April 1, 1866, select one of them as a permanent partner; a farm laborer must "rise at dawn," feed the animals, care for the property, be quiet and orderly, and "retire at reasonable hours"; on Sunday the servants must take turns in doing the necessary work, and they must be respectful and civil to the "master and his family, guests, and agents"; to engage in skilled labor the negro must obtain a license. Whipping and the pillory were permitted in Florida for certain offenses, and in South Carolina the master might "moderately correct" servants under eighteen years of age. Other punishments were generally the same for both races, except the hiring out for petty offenses.

From the Southern point of view none of this

legislation was regarded as a restriction of negro
rights but as a wide extension to the negro of rights
never before possessed, an adaptation of the white
man's laws to his peculiar case. It is doubtful
whether in some of the States the authorities believed that there were any discriminatory laws;
they probably overlooked some of the free negro
legislation already on the statute books. In Alabama, for example, General Wager Swayne, the
head of the Freedmen's Bureau, reported that all
such laws had either been dropped by the legislature or had been vetoed by the governor. Yet
the statute books do show some discriminations.
There is a marked difference between earlier and
later legislation. The more stringent laws were
enacted before the end of 1865. After New Year's
Day had passed and the negroes had begun to
settle down, the legislatures either passed mild
laws or abandoned all special legislation for the
negroes. Later in 1866, several States repealed the
legislation of 1865.

In so far as the "Black Laws" discriminated
against the negro they were never enforced but
were suspended from the beginning by the army
and the Freedmen's Bureau. They had, however, a very important effect upon that section of

7

Northern opinion which was already suspicious of the good faith of the Southerners. They were part of a plan, some believed, to reënslave the negro or at least to create by law a class of serfs. This belief did much to bring about later radical legislation.

If the "Black Laws" represented the reaction of the Southern legislatures to racial conditions, the Freedmen's Bureau was the corresponding result of the interest taken by the North in the welfare of the negro. It was established just as the war was closing and arose out of the various attempts to meet the negro problems that arose during the war. The Bureau had always a dual nature, due in part to its inheritance of regulations, precedents, and traditions from the various attempts made during war time to handle the many thousands of negroes who came under Federal control, and in part to the humanitarian impulses of 1865, born of a belief in the capacity of the negro for freedom and a suspicion that the Southern whites intended to keep as much of slavery as they could. The officials of the Bureau likewise were of two classes: those in control were for the most part army officers, standing as arbiters between white and black, usually just and seldom the victims of their sympathies; but the mass of less responsible officials were men of inferior ability and character, either blind partisans of the negro or corrupt and subject to purchase by the whites.

In view of the fact that the Freedmen's Bureau was considered a new institution in 1865, it is rather remarkable how closely it followed in organization, purpose, and methods the precedents set during the war by the officers of the army and the Treasury. In Virginia, General Butler, in 1861, declared escaped slaves to be "contraband" and proceeded to organize them into communities for discipline, work, food, and care. His successors in Virginia and North Carolina, and others in the Sea Islands of Georgia and South Carolina, extended his plan and arranged a labor system with fixed wages, hours, and methods of work, and everywhere made use of the captured or abandoned property of the Confederates. In Tennessee and Arkansas, Chaplain John Eaton of Grant's army employed thousands in a modified free labor system; and further down in Mississippi and Louisiana Generals Grant, Butler, and Banks also put large numbers of captured slaves to work for themselves and for the Government. Everywhere, as the numbers of negroes increased, the army commanders divided the occupied negro regions into districts under superintendents and other officials, framed labor laws, coöperated with benevolent societies which gave schooling and medical care to the blacks, and developed systems of government for them.

The United States Treasury Department, attempting to execute the confiscation laws for the benefit of the Treasury, appears now and then as an employer of negro labor on abandoned plantations. Either alone or in coöperation with the army and charitable associations, it even supervised negro colonies, and sometimes it assumed practically complete control of the economic welfare of the negro. This Department introduced in 1864 an elaborate lessee and trade system. The negro was regarded as "the ward of the nation," but he was told impressively that "labor is a public duty and idleness and vagrancy a crime." All wanted him to work: the Treasury wanted cotton and other crops to sell; the lessees and speculators wanted to make fortunes by his labor; and the army wanted to be free from the burden of the idle blacks. In spite of all these ministrations the negroes suffered much from harsh treatment, neglect, and unsanitary conditions.

During 1863 and 1864 several influences were

urging the establishment of a national bureau or department to take charge of matters relating to the African race. Some wished to establish on the borders of the South a paid labor system, which might later be extended over the entire region, to get more slaves out of the Confederacy into this free labor territory, and to prevent immigration of negroes into the North, which, after the Emancipation Proclamation, was apprehensive of this danger. Others wished to relieve the army and the treasury officials of the burden of caring for the blacks and to protect the latter from the "northern harpies and bloodhounds" who had fastened upon them the lessee system.

The discussion lasted for two years. The Freedmen's Inquiry Commission, after a survey of the field in 1863, recommended a consolidation of all efforts under an organization which should perpetuate the best features of the old system. But there was much opposition to this plan in Congress. The negroes would be exploited, objected some; the scheme gave too much power to the proposed organization, said others; another objection was urged against the employment of a horde of incompetent and unscrupulous officeholders, for "the men who go down there and become your overseers and negro drivers will be your brokendown politicians and your dilapidated preachers, that description of men who are too lazy to work and just a little too honest to steal."

As the war drew to a close the advocates of a policy of consolidation in negro affairs prevailed, and on March 3, 1865, an act was approved creating in the War Department a Bureau of Refugees, Freedmen, and Abandoned Lands. This Bureau was to continue for one year after the close of the war and it was to control all matters relating to freedmen and refugees, that is, Unionists who had been driven out of the South. Food, shelter, and clothing were to be given to the needy, and abandoned or confiscated property was to be used for or leased to freedmen. At the head of the Bureau was to be a commissioner with an assistant commissioner for each of the Southern States. These officials and other employees must take the "ironclad" oath.

It was planned that the Bureau should have a brief existence, but the institution and its wards became such important factors in politics that on July 16, 1866, after a struggle with the President, Congress passed an act over his veto amplifying the powers of the Bureau and extending it for two

years longer. This continuation of the Bureau
was due to many things: to a belief that former
slaveholders were not to be trusted in dealing with
the negroes; to the baneful effect of the "Black
Laws" upon Northern public opinion; to the struggle between the President and Congress over reconstruction; and to the foresight of radical politicians who saw in the institution an instrument
for the political instruction of the blacks in the
proper doctrines.

The new law was supplementary to the Act of
1865, but its additional provisions merely endorsed
what the Bureau was already doing. It authorized
the issue of medical supplies, confirmed certain
sales of land to negroes, and provided that the
promises which Sherman made in 1865 to the Sea
Island negroes should be carried out as far as
possible and that no lands occupied by blacks
should be restored to the owners until the crops
of 1866 were gathered; it directed the Bureau to
coöperate with private charitable and benevolent
associations, and it authorized the use or sale for
school purposes of all confiscated property; and
finally it ordered that the civil equality of the
negro be upheld by the Bureau and its courts when
state courts refused to accept the principle. By

later laws the existence of the Bureau was extended to January 1, 1869, in the unreconstructed States, but its educational and financial activities were continued until June 20, 1872.

The chief objections to the Bureau from the conservative Northern point of view were summed up in the President's veto messages. The laws creating it were based, he asserted, on the theory that a state of war still existed; there was too great a concentration of power in the hands of a few individuals who could not be held responsible; with such a large number of agents ignorant of the country and often working for their own advantage injustice would inevitably result; in spite of the fact that the negro everywhere had a status in court, arbitrary tribunals were established, without jury, without regular procedure or rules of evidence, and without appeal; the provisions in regard to abandoned lands amounted to confiscation without a hearing; the negro, who must in the end work out his own salvation, and who was protected by the demand for his labor, would be deluded into thinking his future secure without further effort on his part; although nominally under the War Department, the Bureau was not subject to military control; it was practically a great political machine; and, finally, the States most concerned were not represented in Congress.

The Bureau was soon organized in all the former slaveholding States except Delaware, with general headquarters in Washington and state headquarters at the various capitals. General O. O. Howard, who was appointed commissioner, was a good officer, soft-hearted, honest, pious, and frequently referred to as "the Christian soldier." He was fair-minded and not disposed to irritate the Southern whites unnecessarily, but he was rather suspicious of their intentions toward the negroes, and he was a believer in the righteousness of the Freedmen's Bureau. He was not a good business man; and he was not beyond the reach of politicians. At one time he was seriously disturbed in his duties by the buzzing of the presidential bee in his bonnet. The members of his staff were not of his moral stature, and several of them were connected with commercial and political enterprises which left their motives open to criticism.

The assistant commissioners were, as a rule, general officers of the army, though a few were colonels and chaplains.[1] Nearly half of them had

[1] They numbered eleven at first and fourteen after July, 1866, and were changed so often that fifty, in all, served in this rank before January 1, 1869, when the Bureau was practically discontinued.

during the war been associated with the various attempts to handle the negro problem, and it was these men who shaped the organization of the Bureau. While few of them were immediately acceptable to the Southern whites, only ten of them proved seriously objectionable on account of personality, character, or politics. Among the most able should be mentioned Generals Schofield, Swayne, Fullerton, Steedman, and Fessenden, and Colonel John Eaton. The President had little or no control over the appointment or discipline of the officials and agents of the Bureau, except possibly by calling some of the higher army officers back to military service.

As a result of General Grant's severe criticism of the arrangement which removed the Bureau from control by the military establishment, the military commander was in a few instances also appointed assistant commissioner. Each assistant commissioner was aided by a headquarters staff and had under his jurisdiction in each State various district, county, and local agents, with a special corps of school officials, who were usually teachers and missionaries belonging to religious and charitable societies. The local agents were recruited from the members of the Veteran Reserve Corps, the subordinate officers and non-commissioned officers of the army, mustered-out soldiers, officers of negro troops, preachers, teachers, and Northern civilians who had come South. As a class these agents were not competent persons to guide the blacks in the ways of liberty or to arbitrate differences between the races. There were many exceptions, but the Southern view as expressed by General Wade Hampton had only too much foundation: "There *may* be," he said, "an honest man connected with the Bureau." John Minor Botts, a Virginian who had remained loyal to the Union, asserted that many of the agents were good men who did good work but that trouble resulted from the ignorance and fanaticism of others. The minority members of the Ku Klux Committee condemned the agents as being "generally of a class of fanatics without character or responsibility."

The chief activities of the Bureau included the following five branches: relief work for both races; the regulation of negro labor; the administration of justice in cases concerning negroes; the management of abandoned and confiscated property; and the support of schools for the negroes.

The relief work which was carried on for more than four years consisted of caring for sick negroes who were within reach of the hospitals, furnishing food and sometimes clothing and shelter to destitute blacks and whites, and transporting refugees of both races back to their homes. Nearly a hundred hospitals and clinics were established, and half a million patients were treated. This work was greatly needed, especially for the old and the infirm, and it was well done. The transportation of refugees did not reach large proportions, and after 1866 it was entangled in politics. But the issue of supplies in huge quantities brought much needed relief though at the same time a certain amount of demoralization. The Bureau claimed little credit, and is usually given none, for keeping alive during the fall and winter of 1865–1866 thousands of destitute whites. Yet more than a third of the food issued was to whites, and without it many would have starved. Numerous Confederate soldiers on the way home after the surrender were fed by the Bureau, and in the destitute white districts a great deal of suffering was relieved and prevented by its operations. The negroes, dwelling for the most part in regions where labor was in demand, needed relief for a shorter time, but they were attracted in numbers to the towns by free food, and it was difficult to get them back to work. The political value of the free food issues was not generally recognized until later in 1866 and in 1867.

During the first year of the Bureau an important duty of the agents was the supervision of negro labor and the fixing of wages. Both officials and planters generally demanded that contracts be written, approved, and filed in the office of the Bureau. They thought that the negroes would work better if they were thus bound by contracts. The agents usually required that the agreements between employer and laborer cover such points as the nature of the work, the hours, food and clothes, medical attendance, shelter, and wages. To make wages secure, the laborer was given a lien on the crop; to secure the planter from loss, unpaid wages might be forfeited if the laborer failed to keep his part of the contract. When it dawned upon the Bureau authorities that other systems of labor had been or might be developed in the South, they permitted arrangements for the various forms of cash and share renting. But it was everywhere forbidden to place the negroes under "overseers" or to subject them to "unwilling apprenticeship" and "compulsory working out of debts."

The written contract system for laborers did not work out successfully. The negroes at first were expecting quite other fruits of freedom. One Mississippi negro voiced what was doubtless the opinion of many when he declared that he "considered no man free who had to work for a living." Few negroes would contract for more than three months and none for a period beyond January 1, 1866, when they expected a division of lands among the ex-slaves. In spite of the regulations, most worked on oral agreements. In 1866 nearly all employers threw overboard the written contract system for labor and permitted oral agreements. Some States had passed stringent laws for the enforcing of contracts, but in Alabama, Governor Patton vetoed such legislation on the ground that it was not needed. General Swayne, the Bureau chief for the State, endorsed the Governor's action and stated that the negro was protected by his freedom to leave when mistreated, and the planter, by the need on the part of the negro for food and shelter. Negroes, he said, were afraid of contracts and, besides, contracts led to litigation.

In order to safeguard the civil rights of the negroes the Bureau was given authority to establish courts of its own and to supervise the action of state courts in cases to which freedmen were parties. The majority of the assistant commissioners made no attempt to let the state courts handle negro cases but were accustomed to bring all such cases before the Bureau or the provost courts of the army. In Alabama, quite early, and later in North Carolina, Mississippi, and Georgia, the wiser assistant commissioners arranged for the state courts to handle freedmen's cases with the understanding that discriminating laws were to be suspended. General Swayne in so doing declared that he was "unwilling to establish throughout Alabama courts conducted by persons foreign to her citizenship and strangers to her laws." The Bureau courts were informal affairs, consisting usually of one or two administrative officers. There were no jury, no appeal beyond the assistant commissioner, no rules of procedure, and no accepted body of law. In state courts accepted by the Bureau the proceedings in negro cases were conducted in the same manner as for the whites.

The educational work of the Bureau was at first confined to coöperation with such Northern religious and benevolent societies as were organizing schools and churches for the negroes. After the first year the Bureau extended financial aid and undertook a system of supervision over negro schools. The teachers employed were Northern whites and negroes in about equal numbers. Confiscated Confederate property was devoted to negro education, and in several States the assistant commissioners collected fees and percentages of the negroes' wages for the benefit of the schools. In addition the Bureau expended about six million dollars.

The intense dislike which the Southern whites manifested for the Freedmen's Bureau was due in general to their resentment of outside control of domestic affairs and in particular to unavoidable difficulties inherent in the situation. Among the concrete causes of Southern hostility was the attitude of some of the higher officials and many of the lower ones toward the white people. They assumed that the whites were unwilling to accord fair treatment to the blacks in the matter of wages, schools, and justice. An official in Louisiana declared that the whites would exterminate the negroes if the Bureau were removed. A few months later General Fullerton in the same State reported that trouble was caused by those agents who noisily demanded special privileges for the

negro but who objected to any penalties for his
lawlessness and made of the negroes a pampered
class. General Tillson in Georgia predicted the
extinction of the "old time Southerner with his
hate, cruelty, and malice." General Fisk declared that "there are some of the meanest, un-
subjugated and unreconstructed rascally revolu-
tionists in Kentucky that curse the soil of the
country . . . a more select number of vindictive,
pro-slavery, rebellious legislators cannot be found
than a majority of the Kentucky legislature."
There was a disposition to lecture the whites about
their sins in regard to slavery and to point out
to them how far in their general ignorance and
backwardness they fell short of enlightened people.

The Bureau courts were frequently conducted
in an "illegal and oppressive manner," with "decided partiality for the colored people, without regard to justice." For this reason they were suspended for a time in Louisiana and Georgia
by General Steedman and General Fullerton, and
cases were then sent before military courts. Men
of the highest character were dragged before the
Bureau tribunals upon frivolous complaints, were
lectured, abused, ridiculed, and arbitrarily fined
or otherwise punished. The jurisdiction of the

Bureau courts weakened the civil courts and their frequent interference in trivial matters was not conducive to a return to normal conditions.

The inferior agents, not sufficiently under the control of their superiors, were responsible for a great deal of this bad feeling. Many of them held radical opinions as to the relations of the races, and inculcated these views in their courts, in the schools, and in the new negro churches. Some were charged with even causing strikes and other difficulties in order to be bought off by the whites. The tendency of their work was to create in the negroes a pervasive distrust of the whites.

The prevalent delusion in regard to an impending division of the lands among the blacks had its origin in the operation of the war-time confiscation laws, in some of the Bureau legislation, and in General Sherman's Sea Island order, but it was further fostered by the agents until most blacks firmly believed that each head of a family was to get "40 acres and a mule." This belief seriously interfered with industry and resulted also in widespread swindling by rascals who for years made a practice of selling fraudulent deeds to land with red, white, and blue sticks to mark off the bounds of a chosen spot on the former master's plantation. The assistant commissioners labored hard to disabuse the minds of the negroes, but their efforts were often neutralized by the unscrupulous attitude of the agents.

As the contest over reconstruction developed in Washington, the officials of the Bureau soon recognized the political possibilities of their institution. After mid-year of 1866 the Bureau became a political machine for the purpose of organizing the blacks into the Union League, where the rank and file were taught that reënslavement would follow Democratic victories. Nearly all of the Bureau agents aided in the administration of the reconstruction acts in 1867 and in the organization of the new state and local governments and became officials under the new régime. They were the chief agents in capturing the solid negro vote for the Republican party.

Neither of the two plans for guiding the freedmen into a place in the social order — the "Black Laws" and the Freedmen's Bureau — was successful. The former contained a program which was better suited to actual conditions and which might have succeeded if it had been given a fair trial. These laws were a measure of the extent to which the average white would then go in "accepting the situation" so far as the blacks were concerned. And on the whole the recognition of negro rights made in these laws, and made at a time when the whites believed that they were free to handle the situation, was remarkably fair. The negroes lately released from slavery were admitted to the enjoyment of the same rights as the whites as to legal protection of life, liberty, and property, as to education and as to the family relation, limited only by the clear recognition of the principles of political inferiority and social separation. Unhappily this legislation was not put to the test of practical experience because of the Freedmen's Bureau; it was nevertheless skillfully used to arouse the dominant Northern party to a course of action which made impossible any further effort to treat the race problem with due consideration to actual local conditions.

Much of the work of the Freedmen's Bureau was of only temporary benefit to both races. The results of its more permanent work were not generally good. The institution was based upon the assumption that the negro race must be protected from the white race. In its organization and administration it was an impossible combination of

THADDEUS STEVENS

Photograph by Brady.

Gravure, Andersen-Lamb Co. N. Y.

the practical and the theoretical, of opportunism and humanitarianism, of common sense and idealism. It failed to exert a permanently wholesome influence because its lesser agents were not held to strict accountability by their superiors. Under these agents the alienation of the two races began, and the ill feelings then aroused were destined to persist into a long and troubled future.

CHAPTER V

THE VICTORY OF THE RADICALS

THE soldiers who fought through the war to victory or to defeat had been at home nearly two years before the radicals developed sufficient strength to carry through their plans for a revolutionary reconstruction of the Southern States. At the end of the war a majority of the Northern people would have supported a settlement in accordance with Lincoln's policy. Eight months later a majority, but a smaller one, would have supported Johnson's work had it been possible to secure a popular decision on it. How then did the radicals gain the victory over the conservatives? The answer to this question is given by James Ford Rhodes in terms of personalities: "Three men are responsible for the Congressional policy of Reconstruction: Andrew Johnson, by his obstinacy and bad behavior; Thaddeus Stevens, by his vindictiveness and parliamentary tyranny;

Charles Sumner, by his pertinacity in a misguided humanitarianism." The President stood alone in his responsibility, but his chief opponents were the ablest leaders of a resolute band of radicals.

Radicalism did not begin in the Administration of Andrew Johnson. Lincoln had felt its covert opposition throughout the war, but he possessed the faculty of weakening his opponents, while Johnson's conduct usually multiplied the number and the strength of his enemies. At first the radicals criticized Lincoln's policy in regard to slavery, and after the Emancipation Proclamation they shifted their attack to his "ten per cent" plan for organizing the state governments as outlined in the Proclamation of December, 1863. Lincoln's course was distasteful to them because he did not admit the right of Congress to dictate terms, because of his liberal attitude towards former Confederates, and because he was conservative on the negro question. A schism among the Republican supporters of the war was with difficulty averted in 1864, when Frémont threatened to lead the radicals in opposition to the "Union" party of the President and his conservative policy.

The breach was widened by the refusal of Congress to admit representatives from Arkansas and

Louisiana in 1864 and to count the electoral vote of Louisiana and Tennessee in 1865. The passage of the Wade-Davis reconstruction bill in July, 1864, and the protests of its authors after Lincoln's pocket veto called attention to the growing opposition. Severe criticism caused Lincoln to withdraw the propositions which he had made in April, 1865, with regard to the restoration of Virginia. In his last public speech he referred with regret to the growing spirit of vindictiveness toward the South. Much of the opposition to Lincoln's Southern policy was based not on radicalism, that is, not on any desire for a revolutionary change in the South, but upon a belief that Congress and not the Executive should be entrusted with the work of reorganizing the Union. Many congressional leaders were willing to have Congress itself carry through the very policies which Lincoln had advocated; and a majority of the Northern people would have endorsed them without much caring who was to execute them.

The murder of Lincoln, the failure of the radicals to shape Johnson's policy as they had hoped, and the continuing reaction against the excessive expansion of the executive power added strength to the opposition. But it was a long fight before the radical leaders won. Their victory was due to adroit tactics on their own part and to mistakes, bad judgment, and bad manners on the part of the President. When all hope of controlling Johnson had been given up, Thaddeus Stevens and other leaders of similar views began to contrive means to circumvent him. On December 1, 1865, before Congress met, a caucus of radicals held in Washington agreed that a joint committee of the two Houses should be selected to which should be referred matters relating to reconstruction. This plan would thwart the more conservative Senate and gain a desirable delay in which the radicals might develop their campaign. The next day at a caucus of the Union party the plan went through without arousing the suspicion of the supporters of the Administration. Next, through the influence of Stevens, Edward McPherson, the clerk of the House, omitted from the roll call of the House the names of the members from the South. The radical program was then adopted and a week later the Senate concurred in the action of the House as to the appointment of a Joint Committee on Reconstruction.

On the issues before Congress both Houses were split into rather clearly defined factions:

the extreme radicals with such leaders as Stevens, Sumner, Wade, and Boutwell; the moderate Republicans, chief among whom were Fessenden and Trumbull; the administration Republicans led by Raymond, Doolittle, Cowan, and Dixon; and the Democrats, of whom the ablest were Reverdy Johnson, Guthrie, and Hendricks. All except the extreme radicals were willing to support the President or to come to some fairly reasonable compromise. But at no time were they given an opportunity to get together. Johnson and the administration leaders did little in this direction and the radicals made the most skillful use of the divisions among the conservatives.

Whatever final judgment may be passed upon the radical reconstruction policy and its results, there can be no doubt of the political dexterity of those who carried it through. Chief among them was Thaddeus Stevens, vindictive and unscrupulous, filled with hatred of the Southern leaders, bitter in speech and possessing to an extreme degree the faculty of making ridiculous those who opposed him. He advocated confiscation, the proscription or exile of leading whites, the granting of the franchise and of lands to the negroes, and in Southern States the establishment of territorial

governments under the control of Congress.   These
States should, he said, "never be recognized as
capable of acting in the Union . . . until the Constitution shall have been so amended as to make
it what the makers intended, and so as to secure
perpetual ascendency to the party of the Union."

Charles Sumner, the leader of the radicals in the
Senate, was moved less than Stevens by personal
hostility toward the whites of the South, but his
sympathy was reserved entirely for the blacks.
He was unpractical, theoretical, and not troubled
by constitutional scruples.   To him the Declaration of Independence was the supreme law and it
was the duty of Congress to express its principles
in appropriate legislation.   Unlike Stevens, who
had a genuine liking for the negro, Sumner's sympathy for the race was purely intellectual; for the
individual negro he felt repulsion.   His views were
in effect not different from those of Stevens.   And
he was practical enough not to overlook the value
of the negro vote.   "To my mind," he said, "nothing is clearer than the absolute necessity of suffrage for all colored persons in the disorganized
States.   It will not be enough if you give it to those
who read and write; you will not, in this way,
acquire the voting force which you need there for

the protection of unionists, whether white or black. You will not secure the new allies who are essential to the national cause." A leader of the second rank was his colleague Henry Wilson, who was also actuated by a desire for the negro's welfare and for the perpetuation of the Republican party, which he said contained in its ranks "more of moral and intellectual worth than was ever embodied in any political organization in any land . . . created by no man or set of men but brought into being by Almighty God himself . . . and endowed by the Creator with all political power and every office under Heaven." Shellabarger of Ohio was another important figure among the radicals. The following extract from one of his speeches gives an indication of his character and temperament: "They [the Confederates] framed iniquity and universal murder into law. . . . Their pirates burned your unarmed commerce upon every sea. They carved the bones of the dead heroes into ornaments, and drank from goblets made out of their skulls. They poisoned your fountains, put mines under your soldiers' prisons; organized bands whose leaders were concealed in your homes; and commissions ordered the torch and yellow fever to be carried to your cities and to your women and children. They planned one universal bonfire of the North from Lake Ontario to the Missouri."

Among the lesser lights may be mentioned Morton and Wade, both bluff, coarse, and ungenerous, and thoroughly convinced that the Republican party had a monopoly of loyalty, wisdom, and virtues, and that by any means it must gain and keep control; Boutwell, fanatical and mediocre; and Benjamin Butler, a charlatan and demagogue. As a class the Western radicals were less troubled by humanitarian ideals than were those of the East and sought more practical political results.

The Joint Committee on Reconstruction which finally decided the fate of the Southern States was composed of eight radicals, four moderate Republicans, and three Democrats. As James Gillespie Blaine wrote later, "it was foreseen that in an especial degree the fortunes of the Republican party would be in the keeping of the fifteen men who might be chosen." This committee was divided into four subcommittees to take testimony. The witnesses, all of whom were examined at Washington, included army officers and Bureau agents who had served in the South, Southern Unionists, a few politicians, and several former Confederates, among them General Robert E. Lee and Alexander

H. Stephens. Most of the testimony was of the kind needed to support the contentions of the radicals that negroes were badly treated in the South; that the whites were disloyal; that, should they be left in control, the negro, free labor, the nation, and the Republican party would be in danger; that the army and the Freedmen's Bureau must be kept in the South; and that a radical reconstruction was necessary. No serious effort, however, was made to ascertain the actual conditions in the South. Slow to formulate a definite plan, the Joint Committee guided public sentiment toward radicalism, converted gradually the Republican Congressmen, and little by little undermined the power and influence of the President.

Not until after the new year was it plain that there was to be a fight to the finish between Congress and the President. Congress had refused in December, 1865, to accept the President's program, but there was still hope for a compromise. Many conservatives had voted for the delay merely to assert the rights of Congress; but the radicals wanted time to frame a program. The Northern Democrats were embarrassingly cordial in their support of Johnson and so also were most Southerners. The moderates were not far away

from the position of the President and the administration Republicans. But the radicals skillfully
postponed a test of strength until Stevens and
Sumner were ready. The latter declared that a
generation must elapse "before the rebel communities have so far been changed as to become
safe associates in a common government. Time,
therefore, we must have. Through time all other
guarantees may be obtained; but time itself is
a guarantee."

To the Joint Committee were referred without
debate all measures relating to reconstruction, but
the Committee was purposely making little progress — contented merely to take testimony and to
act as a clearing house for the radical "facts"
about "Southern outrages" while waiting for the
tide to turn. The "Black Laws" and the election
of popular Confederate leaders to office in the
South were effectively used to alarm the friends
of the negroes, and the reports from the Bureau
agents gave support to those who condemned the
Southern state governments as totally inadequate
and disloyal.

So apparent was the growth of radicalism that
the President, alarmed by the attitude of Sumner
and Stevens and their followers, began to fear for

the Constitution and forced the fight. The passage of a bill on February 6, 1866, extending the life of the Freedmen's Bureau furnished the occasion for the beginning of the open struggle. On the 19th of February Johnson vetoed the bill, and the next day an effort was made to pass it over the veto. Not succeeding in this attempt, the House of Representatives adopted a concurrent resolution that Senators and Representatives from the Southern States should be excluded until Congress declared them entitled to representation. Ten days later the Senate also adopted the resolution.

Though it was not yet too late for Johnson to meet the conservatives of Congress on middle ground, he threw away his opportunity by an intemperate and undignified speech on the 22d of February to a crowd at the White House. As usual when excited, he forgot the proprieties and denounced the radicals as enemies of the Union and even went so far as to charge Stevens, Sumner, and Wendell Phillips with endeavoring to destroy the fundamental principles of the government. Such conduct weakened his supporters and rejoiced his enemies. It was expected that Johnson would approve the bill to confer civil rights upon the negroes, but, goaded perhaps by the speeches of Stevens, he vetoed it on the 27th of March. Its patience now exhausted, Congress passed the bill over the President's veto. To secure the requisite majority in the Senate, Stockton, Democratic Senator from New Jersey, was unseated on technical grounds, and Senator Morgan, who was "paired" with a sick colleague, broke his word to vote aye — for which Wade offensively thanked God. The moderates had now fallen away from the President and at least for this session of Congress his policies were wrecked. On the 16th of July the supplementary Freedmen's Bureau Act was passed over the veto, and on the 24th of July Tennessee was readmitted to representation by a law the preamble of which asserted unmistakably that Congress had assumed control of reconstruction.

Meanwhile the Joint Committee on Reconstruction had made a report asserting that the Southerners had forfeited all constitutional rights, that their state governments were not in constitutional form, and that restoration could be accomplished only when Congress and the President acted together in fixing the terms of readmission. The uncompromising hostility of the South, the Committee asserted, made necessary adequate safeguards which should include the disfranchisement

8

of the white leaders, either negro suffrage or a reduction of white representation, and repudiation of the Confederate war debt with recognition of the validity of the United States debt. These terms were embodied in the Fourteenth Amendment, which was adopted by Congress and sent to the States on June 13, 1866.

In the congressional campaign of 1866 reconstruction was almost the sole issue. For success the Administration must gain at least one-third of one house, while the radicals were fighting for two-thirds of each House. If the Administration should fail to make the necessary gain, the work accomplished by the Presidents would be destroyed. The campaign was bitter and extended through the summer and fall. Four national conventions were held: the National Union party at Philadelphia made a respectable showing in support of the President; the Southern Unionists, guided by the Northern radicals met at the same place; a soldiers' and sailors' convention at Cleveland supported the Administration; and another convention of soldiers and sailors at Pittsburgh endorsed the radical policies. A convention of Confederate soldiers and sailors at Memphis endorsed the President, but the Southern support and that of the Northern Democrats did not encourage moderate Republicans to vote for the Administration. Three members of Johnson's Cabinet — Harlan, Speed, and Dennison — resigned because they were unwilling to follow their chief further in opposing Congress.

The radicals had plenty of campaign material in the testimony collected by the Joint Committee, in the reports of the Freedmen's Bureau, and in the bloody race riots which had occurred in Memphis and New Orleans. The greatest blunder of the Administration was Johnson's speechmaking tour to the West which he called "Swinging Around the Circle." Every time he made a speech he was heckled by persons in the crowd, lost his temper, denounced Congress and the radical leaders, and conducted himself in an undignified manner. The election returns showed more than a two-thirds majority in each House against the President. The Fortieth Congress would therefore be safely radical, and in consequence the Thirty-ninth was encouraged to be more radical during its last session.

Public interest now for a time turned to the South, where the Fourteenth Amendment was before the state legislatures. The radicals, taunted with having no plan of reconstruction beyond a desire to keep the Southern States out of the Union, professed to see in the ratification of the Fourteenth Amendment a good opportunity to readmit the States on a safe basis. The elections of 1866 had pointed to the ratification of the proposed amendment as an essential preliminary to readmission. But would additional demands be made upon the South? Sumner, Stevens, and Fessenden were sure that negro suffrage also must come, but Wade, Chase, Garfield, and others believed that nothing beyond the terms of the Fourteenth Amendment would be asked.

In the Southern legislatures there was little disposition to ratify the amendment. The rapid development of the radical policies during 1866 had convinced most Southerners that nothing short of a general humiliation and complete revolution in the South would satisfy the dominant party, and there were few who wished to be "parties to our own dishonor." The President advised the States not to accept the amendment, but several Southern leaders favored it, fearing that worse would come if they should reject it. Only in the legislatures of Alabama and Florida was there any serious disposition to accept the amendment; and in the end all the unreconstructed States voted adversely

during the fall and winter of 1866–67. This una-
nimity of action was due in part to the belief that,
even if the amendment were ratified, the Southern
States would still be excluded, and in part to the
general dislike of the proscriptive section which
would disfranchise all Confederates of prominence
and result in the breaking up of the state governments. The example of unhappy Tennessee,
which had ratified the Fourteenth Amendment and
had been readmitted, was not one to encourage
conservative people in the other Southern States.

The rejection of the amendment put the question of reconstruction squarely before Congress.
There was no longer a possibility of accomplishing
the reconstruction of the Southern States by means
of constitutional amendments. Some of the Border
and Northern States were already showing signs
of uneasiness at the continued exclusion of the
South. But if the Constitutional Amendment had
failed, other means of reconstruction were at hand,
for the radicals now controlled the Thirty-ninth
Congress, from which the Southern representatives were excluded, and would also control the
Fortieth Congress.

Under the lead of Stevens and Sumner the radicals now perfected their plans. On January 8, 1867,

their first measure, conferring the franchise upon negroes in the District of Columbia, was passed over the presidential veto, though the proposal had been voted down a few weeks earlier by a vote of 6525 to 35 in Washington and 812 to 1 in Georgetown. In the next place, by an act of January 31, 1867, the franchise was extended to negroes in the territories, and on March 2, 1867, three important measures were enacted: the Tenure of Office Act and a rider to the Army Appropriation Act — both designed to limit the power of the President — and the first Reconstruction Act. By the Tenure of Office Act the President was prohibited from removing officeholders except with the consent of the Senate; and by the Army Act he was forbidden to issue orders except through General Grant or to relieve him of command or to assign him to command away from Washington unless at the General's own request or with the previous approval of the Senate.   The first measure was meant to check the removal of radical officeholders by Johnson, and the other, which was secretly drawn up for Boutwell by Stanton, was designed to prevent the President from exercising his constitutional command of the army.

The first Reconstruction Act declared that no

legal state government existed in the ten unreconstructed States and that there was no adequate
protection for life and property. The Johnson and
Lincoln governments in those States were declared
to have no legal status and to be subject wholly to
the authority of the United States to modify or
abolish. The ten States were divided into five
military districts, over each of which a general
officer was to be placed in command. Military
tribunals were to supersede the civil courts where
necessary. Stevens was willing to rest here,
though some of his less radical followers, disliking
military rule but desiring to force negro suffrage,
inserted a provision in the law that a State might
be readmitted to representation upon the following
conditions: a constitutional convention must be
held, the members of which were elected by males
of voting age without regard to color, excluding
whites who would be disfranchised by the proposed
Fourteenth Amendment; a constitution including
the same rule of suffrage must be framed, ratified
by the same electorate, and approved by Congress; and lastly, the legislatures elected under this
constitution must ratify the proposed Fourteenth
Amendment, after which, if the Fourteenth Amendment should have become a part of the Federal

Constitution, the State should be readmitted to representation.

In order that the administration of this radical legislation might be supervised by its friends, the Thirty-ninth Congress had passed a law requiring the Fortieth Congress to meet on the 4th of March instead of in December as was customary. According to the Reconstruction Act of the 2d of March it was left to the state government or to the people of a State to make the first move towards reconstruction. If they preferred, they might remain under military rule. Either by design or by carelessness no machinery of administration was provided for the execution of the act. When it became evident that the Southerners preferred military rule the new Congress passed a Supplementary Reconstruction Act on the 23d of March designed to force the earlier act into operation. The five commanding generals were directed to register the blacks of voting age and the whites who were not disfranchised, to hold elections for conventions, to call the conventions, to hold elections to ratify or reject the constitutions, and to forward the constitutions, if ratified, to the President for transmission to Congress.

In these reconstruction acts the whole doctrine

of radicalism was put on the way to accomplishment. Its spread had been rapid. In December, 1865, the majority of Congress would have accepted with little modification the work of Lincoln and Johnson. Three months later the Civil Rights Act measured the advance. Very soon the new Freedmen's Bureau Act and the Fourteenth Amendment indicated the rising tide of radicalism. The campaign of 1866 and the attitude of the Southern States swept all radicals and most moderate Republicans swiftly into a merciless course of reconstruction. Moderate reconstruction had nowhere strong support. Congress, touched in its *amour propre* by presidential disregard, was eager for extremes. Johnson, who regarded himself as defending the Constitution against radical assaults, was stubborn, irascible, and undignified, and with his associates was no match in political strategy for his radical opponents.

The average Republican or Unionist in the North, if he had not been brought by skillful misrepresentation to believe a new rebellion impending in the South, was at any rate painfully alive to the fear that the Democratic party might regain power. With the freeing of the slaves the representation of the South in Congress would be increased. At first it seemed that the South might divide in politics as before the war, but the longer the delay the more the Southern whites tended to unite into one party acting with the Democrats. With their eighty-five representatives and a slight reaction in the North, they might gain control of the lower House of Congress. The Union-Republican party had a majority of less than one hundred in 1866 and this was lessened slightly in the Fortieth Congress. The President was for all practical purposes a Democrat again. The prospect was too much for the very human politicians to view without distress. Stevens, speaking in support of the Military Reconstruction Bill, said:

There are several good reasons for the passage of this bill. In the first place, it is just. I am now confining my argument to negro suffrage in the rebel States. Have not loyal blacks quite as good a right to choose rulers and make laws as rebel whites? In the second place, it is necessary in order to protect the loyal white men in the seceded States. With them the blacks would act in a body, and it is believed that in each of these States, except one, the two united would form a majority, control the States, and protect themselves. Now they are the victims of daily murder. They must suffer constant persecution or be exiled. Another good reason is that it would insure the ascendency of the union party. . . . I believe . . . that on the continued ascendency of that party depends the safety of this great nation. If impartial suffrage is excluded in the rebel States, then every one of them is sure to send a solid rebel electoral vote. They, with their kindred Copperheads of the North, would always elect the President and control Congress.

The laws passed on the 2d and the 23d of March were war measures and presupposed a continuance of war conditions. The Lincoln-Johnson state governments were overturned; Congress fixed the qualifications of voters for that time and for the future; and the President, shorn of much of his constitutional power, could exercise but little control over the military government. Nothing that a State might do would secure restoration until it should ratify the Fourteenth Amendment to the Federal Constitution. The war had been fought upon the theory that the old Union must be preserved; but the basic theory of the reconstruction was that a new Union was to be created.

CHAPTER VI

THE RULE OF THE MAJOR GENERALS

FROM the passage of the reconstruction acts to the close of Johnson's Administration, Congress, working the will of the radical majority, was in supreme control. The army carried out the will of Congress and to that body, not to the President, the commanding general and his subordinates looked for direction.

The official opposition of the President to the policy of Congress ceased when that policy was enacted into law. He believed this legislation to be unconstitutional, but he considered it his duty to execute the laws. He at once set about the appointment of generals to command the military districts created in the South,[1] a task

---

[1] The first five generals appointed were Schofield, Sickles, Pope, Ord, and Sheridan. None of these remained in his district until reconstruction was completed. To Schofield's command in the first district succeeded in turn Stoneman, Webb, and Canby; Sickles gave way to Canby, and Pope to Meade; Ord in the fourth district was

calling for no little discretion, since much depended upon the character of these military governors, or "satraps," as they were frequently called by the opposition. The commanding general in a district was charged with many duties, military, political, and administrative. It was his duty to carry on a government satisfactory to the radicals and not too irritating to the Southern whites; at the same time he must execute the reconstruction acts by putting old leaders out of power and negroes in. Violent opposition to this policy on the part of the South was not looked for. Notwithstanding the "Southern outrage" campaign, it was generally recognized in government circles that conditions in the seceded States had gradually been growing better since the close of the war. There was in many regions, to be sure, a general laxity in enforcing laws, but that had always been characteristic of the newer parts of the South. The Civil Rights Act was generally in force, the "Black Laws" had been suspended, and

---

followed by Gillem, McDowell, and Ames; Sheridan, in the fifth, was succeeded by Griffen, Mower, Hancock, Buchanan, Reynolds, and Canby. Some of the generals were radical; others, moderate and tactful. The most extreme were Sheridan, Pope, and Sickles. Those most acceptable to the whites were Hancock, Schofield, and Meade. General Grant himself became more radical in his actions as he became involved in the fight between Congress and the President.

the Freedmen's Bureau was everywhere caring for the negroes. What disorder existed was of recent origin and in the main was due to the unsettling effects of the debates in Congress and to the organization of the negroes for political purposes.

Military rule was established in the South with slight friction, but it was soon found that the reconstruction laws were not sufficiently clear on two points: first, whether there was any limit to the authority of the five generals over the local and state governments and, if so, whether the limiting authority was in the President; and second, whether the disfranchising provisions in the laws were punitive and hence to be construed strictly. Attorney-General Stanbery, in May and June, 1867, drew up opinions in which he maintained that the laws were to be considered punitive and therefore to be construed strictly. After discussions in cabinet meetings these opinions received the approval of all except Stanton, Secretary of War, who had already joined the radical camp. The Attorney-General's opinion was sent out to the district commanders for their information and guidance. But Congress did not intend to permit the President or his Cabinet to direct the process of reconstruction, and in the Act of

July 19, 1867, it gave a radical interpretation to the reconstruction legislation, declared itself in control, gave full power to General Grant and to the district commanders subject only to Grant, directed the removal of all local officials who opposed the reconstruction policies, and warned the civil and military officers of the United States that none of them should "be bound in his action by any opinion of any civil officer of the United States." This interpretive legislation gave a broad basis for the military government and resulted in a severe application of the disfranchising provisions of the laws.

The rule of the five generals lasted in all the States until June, 1868, and continued in Mississippi, Texas, Virginia, and Georgia until 1870. There had been, to be sure, some military government in 1865, subject, however, to the President, and from 1865 to 1867 the army, along with the Freedmen's Bureau, had exerted a strong influence in the government of the South, but in the régime now inaugurated the military was supreme. The generals had a superior at Washington, but whether it was the President, General Grant, or Congress was not clear until the Act of July 19, 1867 made Congress the source of authority.

The power of the generals most strikingly appeared in their control of the state governments which were continued as provisional organizations. Since no elections were permitted, all appointments and removals were made from military headquarters, which soon became political beehives, centers of wirepulling and agencies for the distribution of spoils. At the outset civil officers were ordered to retain their offices during good behavior, subject to military control. But no local official was permitted to use his influence ever so slightly against reconstruction. Since most of them did not favor the policy of Congress, thousands were removed as "obstacles to reconstruction." The Governors of Georgia, Louisiana, Virginia, Mississippi, and Texas were displaced and others appointed in their stead. All kinds of subordinate offices rapidly became vacant. New appointments were nearly always carpetbaggers and native radicals who could take the "ironclad" oath. The generals complained that there were not enough competent native "loyalists" to fill the offices, and frequently an army officer was installed as governor, treasurer, secretary of state, auditor, or mayor. In nearly all towns the police force was reorganized and former Federal soldiers were added to the force, while the regular troops were used for general police purposes and for rural constabulary.

Over the administration of justice the military authorities exercised a close supervision. Instructions were sent out to court officers covering the selection of juries, the suspension of certain laws, and the rules of evidence and procedure. Courts were often closed, court decrees set aside or modified, prisoners released, and many cases reserved for trial by military commission. Some commanders required juries to admit negro members and insisted that all jurors take the "ironclad" test oath. There was some attempt at regulating the Federal courts but without much success.

Since the state legislatures were forbidden to meet, much legislation was enacted through military orders. Stay laws were enacted, the color line was abolished, new criminal regulations were promulgated, and the police power was invoked in some instances to justify sweeping measures, such as the prohibition of whisky manufacture in North Carolina and South Carolina. The military governors levied, increased, or decreased taxes and made appropriations which the state treasurers were forced to pay, but they restrained the radical conventions, all of which wished to spend much money.

10

According to the Act of March 23, 1867, the generals and their appointees were to be paid by the United States, but in practice the running expenses of reconstruction were paid by the state treasurers.

Any attempt to favor the Confederate soldiers was frowned upon. Laws providing wooden legs and free education for crippled Confederates were suspended. Militia organizations and military schools were forbidden. No uniform might be worn, no parades were permitted, no memorial and historical societies were to be organized, and no meeting of any kind could be held without a permit. The attempt to control the press resulted in what one general called "a horrible uproar." Editors were forbidden to express themselves too strongly against reconstruction; public advertising and printing were awarded only to those papers actively supporting reconstruction. Several newspapers were suppressed, a notable example being the *Tuscaloosa Independent Monitor*, whose editor, Ryland Randolph, was a picturesque figure in Alabama journalism and a leader in the Ku Klux Klan.

The military administration was thorough, and as a whole honest and efficient. With fewer than ten thousand soldiers the generals maintained order and carried on the reconstruction of the South. The whites made no attempt at resistance, though they were irritated by military rule and resented the loss of self-government. But most Southerners preferred the rule of the army to the alternative reign of the carpetbagger, scalawag, and negro. The extreme radicals at the North, on the other hand, were disgusted at the conservative policy of the generals. The apathy of the whites at the beginning of the military reconstruction excited surprise on all sides. Not only was there no violent opposition, but for a few weeks there was no opposition at all. The civil officials were openly unsympathetic, and the newspapers voiced dissent not untouched with disgust; others simply could not take the situation seriously because it seemed so absurd; many leaders were indifferent, while others — among them, Generals Lee, Beauregard, and Longstreet, and Governor Patton — without approving the policy, advised the whites to coöperate with the military authorities and save all they could out of the situation. General Beauregard, for instance, wrote in 1867: "If the suffrage of the negro is properly handled and directed we shall defeat our adversaries with their own weapons. The negro is Southern born.   With education and property qualifications he can be made to take an interest in the affairs of the South and in its prosperity. He will side with the whites."

Northern observers who were friendly to the South or who disapproved of this radical reconstruction saw the danger more clearly than the Southerners themselves, who seemed not to appreciate the full implication of the situation.   In this connection the New York *Herald* remarked:

We may regard the entire ten unreconstructed Southern States, with possibly one or two exceptions, as forced by a secret and overwhelming revolutionary influence to a common and inevitable fate.   They are all bound to be governed by blacks spurred on by worse than blacks — white wretches who dare not show their faces in respectable society anywhere.   This is the most abominable phase barbarism has assumed since the dawn of civilization.   It was all right and proper to put down the rebellion.   It was all right perhaps to emancipate the slaves. . . .   But it is not right to make slaves of white men even though they may have been former masters of blacks.   This is but a change in a system of bondage that is rendered the more odious and intolerable because it has been inaugurated in an enlightened instead of a dark and uncivilized age.

The political parties rapidly grouped themselves for the coming struggle.   The radical Republican party indeed was in process of organization in the South even before the passage of the reconstruction acts. Its membership was made up of negroes, carpetbaggers, or Northern men who had come in as speculators, officers of the Freedmen's Bureau and of the army, scalawags or Confederate renegades, "Peace Society" men,[1] and Unionists of Civil War times, with a few old Whigs who could not yet bring themselves to affiliate with the Democrats. At first it seemed that a respectable number of whites might be secured for the radical party, but the rapid organization of the negroes checked the accession of whites. In the winter and spring of 1866–67 the negroes near the towns were well organized by the Union League and the Freedmen's Bureau and then, after the passage of the reconstruction acts, the organizing activities of the radical chieftains shifted to the rural districts. The Union League was greatly extended; Union League conventions were held to which local whites were not admitted; and the formation of a black man's party was well on the way before the registration of the voters was completed. Visiting statesmen from the North, among them

[1] See *The Day of the Confederacy,* by Nathaniel W. Stephenson (in *The Chronicles of America*), p. 121, footnote.

Henry Wilson of Massachusetts and "Pig Iron" Kelley of Pennsylvania, toured the South in support of the radical program, and the registrars and all Federal officials aided in the work.

The whites, slow to comprehend the real extent of radicalism, were finally aroused to the necessity of organizing, if they were to influence the negro and have a voice in the conventions. The old party divisions were still evident. With difficulty a portion of the Whigs were brought with the Democrats into one conservative party during the summer and fall of 1867, though many still held aloof. The lack of the old skilled leadership was severely felt. In places where the white man's party was given a name it was called "Democratic *and* Conservative," to spare the feelings of former Whigs who were loath to bear the party name of their quondam opponents.

The first step in the military reconstruction was the registration of voters. In each State a central board of registrars was appointed by the district commander and a local board for every county and large town. Each board consisted of three members — all radicals — who were required to subscribe to the "ironclad" oath. In several States one negro was appointed to each local board. The registrars listed negro voters during the day, and at night worked at the organization of a radical Republican party. The prospective voters were required to take the oath prescribed in the Reconstruction Act, but the registrars were empowered to go behind the oath and investigate the Confederate record of each applicant. This authority was invoked to carry the disfranchisement of the whites far beyond the intention of the law in an attempt to destroy the leadership of the whites and to register enough negroes to outvote them at the polls. For this purpose the registration was continued until October 1, 1867, and an active campaign of education and organization carried on.

At the close of the registration 703,000 black voters were on the rolls and 627,000 whites. In Alabama, Louisiana, South Carolina, Florida, and Mississippi there were black majorities, and in the other States the blacks and the radical whites together formed majorities. The white minorities included several thousand who had been rejected by the registrars but restored by the military commanders. Though large numbers of blacks were dropped from the revised rolls as fraudulently registered, the registration statistics nevertheless bore clear witness to the political purpose of those who compiled them.

Next followed a vote on the question of holding a state convention and the election of delegates to such a convention if held — a double election. The whites, who had been harassed in the registration and who feared race conflicts at the elections, considered whether they ought not to abstain from voting. By staying away from the polls, they might bring the vote cast in each State below a majority and thus defeat the proposed conventions for, unless a majority of the registered voters actually cast ballots either for or against a convention, no convention could be held. Nowhere, however, was this plan of not voting fully carried out, for, though most whites abstained, enough of them voted (against the conventions, of course) to make the necessary majority in each State. The effect of the abstention policy upon the personnel of the conventions was unfortunate. In every convention there was a radical majority with a conservative and all but negligible minority. In South Carolina and Louisiana there were negro majorities. In every State except North Carolina, Texas, and Virginia the negroes and the carpetbaggers together were in the majority over native whites.

The conservative whites were of fair ability; the carpetbaggers and scalawags produced in each convention a few able leaders, but most of them were conscienceless political soldiers of fortune; the negro members were inexperienced, and most of them were quite ignorant, though a few leaders of ability did appear among them. In Alabama, for example, only two negro members could write, though half had been taught to sign their names. They were barbers, field hands, hack drivers, and servants. A negro chaplain was elected who invoked divine blessings on "unioners and cusses on rebels." It was a sign of the new era when the convention specially invited the "ladies of colored members" to seats in the gallery.

The work of the conventions was for the most part cut and dried, the abler members having reached a general agreement before they met. The constitutions, mosaics of those of other States, were noteworthy only for the provisions made to keep the whites out of power and to regulate the relations of the races in social matters. The Texas constitution alone contained no proscriptive clauses beyond those required by the Fourteenth Amendment. The most thoroughgoing proscription of Confederates was found in the constitutions of Mississippi, Alabama, and Virginia; and in these States the voter must also purge himself of guilt by agreeing to accept the "civil and political equality of all men" or by supporting reconstruction. Only in South Carolina and Louisiana were race lines abolished by law.

The legislative work of the conventions was more interesting than the constitution making. By ordinance the legality of negro marriages was dated from November, 1867, or some date later than had been fixed by the white conventions of 1865. Mixed schools were provided in some States; militia for the black districts but not for the white was to be raised; while in South Carolina it was made a penal offense to call a person a "Yankee" or a "nigger." Few of the negro delegates demanded proscription of whites or social equality; they wanted schools and the vote. The white radicals were more anxious to keep the former Confederates from holding office than from voting. The generals in command everywhere used their influence to secure moderate action by the conventions, and for this they were showered with abuse.

As provided by the reconstruction acts, the new constitutions were submitted to the electorate created by those instruments. Unless a majority of the registered voters in a State should take part in the election the reconstruction would fail and the State would remain under military rule. The whites now inaugurated a more systematic policy of abstention and in Alabama, on February 4, 1868, succeeded in holding the total vote below a majority. Congress then rushed to the rescue of radicalism with the act of the 11th of March, which provided that a mere majority of those voting in the State was sufficient to inaugurate reconstruction. Arkansas had followed the lead of Alabama, but too late; in Mississippi the constitution was defeated by a majority vote; in Texas the convention had made no provision for a vote; and in Virginia the commanding general, disapproving of the work of the convention, refused to pay the expenses of an election. In the other six States the constitutions were adopted.[1]

These elections gave rise to more violent contests than before. They also were double elections, as the voters cast ballots for state and local officials and at the same time for or against the constitution. The radical nominations were made by the

[1] Except in Texas, the work of constitution making was completed between November 5, 1867, and May 18, 1868.

Union League and the Freedmen's Bureau, and
nearly all radicals who had been members of conventions were nominated and elected to office.
The negroes, expecting now to reap some benefits
of reconstruction, frequently brought sacks to the
polls to "put the franchise in." The elections were
all over by June, 1868, and the newly elected legislatures promptly ratified the Fourteenth Amendment.

It now remained for Congress to approve the
work done in the South and to readmit the reorganized States. The case of Alabama gave some
trouble. Even Stevens, for a time, thought that
this State should stay out; but there was danger
in delay. The success of the abstention policy in
Alabama and Arkansas and the reviving interest
of the whites foreshadowed white majorities in
some places; the scalawags began to forsake the
radical party for the conservatives; and there were
Democratic gains in the North in 1867. Only six
States, New York and five New England States,
allowed the negro to vote, while four States, Minnesota, Michigan, Kansas, and Ohio, voted down
negro suffrage after the passage of the reconstruction acts. The ascendancy of the radicals in Congress was menaced. The radicals needed the support of their radical brethren in Southern States

and they could not afford to wait for the Fourteenth Amendment to become a part of the Constitution or to tolerate other delay. On the 22d and the 25th of June acts were therefore passed admitting seven States, Alabama included, to representation in Congress upon the "fundamental condition" that "the constitutions of neither of said States shall ever be so amended or changed as to deprive any citizens or class of citizens of the United States of the right to vote in said State, who are entitled to vote by the constitution thereof herein recognized."

The generals now turned over the government to the recently elected radical officials and retired into the background. Military reconstruction was thus accomplished in all the States except Virginia, Mississippi, and Texas.

CHAPTER VII

THE TRIAL OF PRESIDENT JOHNSON

WHILE the radical program was being executed in the South, Congress was engaged not only in supervising reconstruction but in subduing the Supreme Court and in "conquering" President Johnson. One must admire the efficiency of the radical machine. When the Southerners showed that they preferred military rule as permitted by the Act of the 2d of March, Congress passed the Act of the 23d of March which forced the reconstruction. When the President ventured to assert his power in behalf of a considerate administration of the reconstruction acts, Congress took the power out of his hands by the law of the 19th of July. The Southern plan to defeat the new state constitutions by abstention was no sooner made clear in the case of Alabama than Congress came to the rescue with the Act of March 11, 1868.

Had it seemed necessary, Congress would have

handled the Supreme Court as it did the Southerners. The opponents of radical reconstruction were anxious to get the reconstruction laws of March, 1867, before the Court. Chief Justice Chase was known to be opposed to military reconstruction, and four other justices were, it was believed, doubtful of the constitutionality of the laws. A series of conservative decisions gave hope to those who looked to the Court for relief. The first decision, in the case of *ex parte* Milligan, declared unconstitutional the trials of civilians by military commissions when civil courts were open. A few months later, in the cases of Cummings *vs.* Missouri and *ex parte* Garland, the Court declared invalid, because *ex post facto*, the state laws designed to punish former Confederates.

But the first attempts to get the reconstruction acts before the Supreme Court failed. The State of Mississippi, in April, 1867, brought suit to restrain the President from executing the reconstruction acts. The Court refused to interfere with the Executive. A similar suit was then brought against Secretary Stanton by Georgia with a like result. But in 1868, in the case of *ex parte* McCardle, it appeared that the question of the constitutionality of the reconstruction acts would be passed upon. McCardle, a Mississippi editor arrested for opposition to reconstruction and convicted by military commission, appealed to the Supreme Court, which asserted its jurisdiction. But the radicals in alarm rushed through Congress an act (March 27, 1868) which took away from the Court its jurisdiction in cases arising under the reconstruction acts. The highest court was thus silenced.

The attempt to remove the President from office was the only part of the radical program that failed, and this by the narrowest of margins. During the spring and summer of 1866 there was some talk among politicians of impeaching President Johnson, and in December a resolution was introduced by Representative Ashley of Ohio looking toward impeachment. Though the committee charged with the investigation of "the official conduct of Andrew Johnson" reported that enough testimony had been taken to justify further inquiry, the House took no action. There were no less than five attempts at impeachment during the next year. Stevens, Butler, and others were anxious to get the President out of the way, but the majority were as yet unwilling to impeach for merely political reasons. There were some who thought that the radicals had sufficient majorities to ensure all needed legislation and did not relish the thought of Ben Wade in the presidency.[1] Others considered that no just grounds for action had been found in the several investigations of Johnson's record. Besides, the President's authority and influence had been much curtailed by the legislation relating to the Freedmen's Bureau, tenure of office, reconstruction, and command of the army, and Congress had also refused to recognize his amnesty and pardoning powers.

But the desire to impeach the President was increasing in power, and very little was needed to provoke a trial of strength between the radicals and the President. The drift toward impeachment was due in part to the legislative reaction against the Executive, and in part to Johnson's own opposition to reconstruction and to his use of the patronage against the radicals. Specific grievances were found in his vetoes of the various reconstruction bills, in his criticisms of Congress and the radical leaders, and in the fact, as Stevens asserted, that he was a "radical renegade."

---

[1] Senator Wade of Ohio was President *pro tempore* of the Senate and by the act of 1791 would succeed President Johnson if he were removed from office.

Johnson was a Southern man, an old-line State Rights Democrat, somewhat anti-negro in feeling. He knew no book except the Constitution, and that he loved with all his soul. Sure of the correctness of his position, he was too stubborn to change or to compromise. He was no more to be moved than Stevens or Sumner. To overcome Johnson's vetoes required two-thirds of each House of Congress; to impeach and remove him would require only a majority of the House and two-thirds of the Senate.

The desired occasion for impeachment was furnished by Johnson's attempt to get Edwin M. Stanton, the Secretary of War, out of the Cabinet. Stanton held radical views and was at no time sympathetic with or loyal to Johnson, but he loved office too well to resign along with those cabinet members who could not follow the President in his struggle with Congress. He was seldom frank and sincere in his dealings with the President, and kept up an underhand correspondence with the radical leaders, even assisting in framing some of the reconstruction legislation which was designed to render Johnson powerless. In him the radicals had a representative within the President's Cabinet.

Wearied of Stanton's disloyalty, Johnson asked him to resign and, upon a refusal, suspended him in August, 1867, and placed General Grant in temporary charge of the War Department. General Grant, Chief Justice Chase, and Secretary McCulloch, though they all disliked Stanton, advised the President against suspending him. But Johnson was determined. About the same time he exercised his power in removing Sheridan and Sickles from their commands in the South and replaced them with Hancock and Canby. The radicals were furious, but Johnson had secured at least the support of a loyal Cabinet.

The suspension of Stanton was reported to the Senate in December, 1867, and on January 13, 1868, the Senate voted not to concur in the President's action. Upon receiving notice of the vote in the Senate, Grant at once left the War Department and Stanton again took possession. Johnson now charged Grant with failing to keep a promise either to hold on himself or to make it possible to appoint some one else who would hold on until the matter might be brought into the courts. The President by this accusation angered Grant and threw him with his great influence into the arms of the radicals.

Against the advice of his leading counselors Johnson persisted in his intention to keep Stanton out of the Cabinet. Accordingly on the 21st of February he dismissed Stanton from office and appointed Lorenzo Thomas, the Adjutant General, as acting Secretary of War. Stanton, advised by the radicals in Congress to "stick," refused to yield possession to Thomas and had him arrested for violation of the Tenure of Office Act. The matter now was in the courts where Johnson wanted it, but the radical leaders, fearing that the courts would decide against Stanton and the reconstruction acts, had the charges against Thomas withdrawn. Thus failed the last attempt to get the reconstruction laws before the courts. On the 22d of February the President sent to the Senate the name of Thomas Ewing, General Sherman's father-in-law, as Secretary of War, but no attention was paid to the nomination.

On February 24, 1868, the House voted, 128 to 47, to impeach the President "of high crimes and misdemeanors in office." The Senate was formally notified the next day and on the 4th of March the seven managers selected by the House appeared before the Senate with the eleven articles of impeachment. At first it seemed to the public

PRESIDENT GRANT

Photograph. In the collection of L. C. Handy, Washington.

Gravure, Anderson-Lamb. Co.N.Y.

that the impeachment proceedings were merely the culmination of a struggle for the control of the army. There were rumors that Johnson had plans to use the army against Congress and against reconstruction. General Grant, directed by Johnson to accept orders from Stanton only if he were satisfied that they came from the President, refused to follow these instructions. Stanton, professing to fear violence, barricaded himself in the War Department and was furnished with a guard of soldiers by General Grant, who from this time used his influence in favor of impeachment. Excited by the most sensational rumors, some people even believed a new rebellion to be imminent.

The impeachment was rushed to trial by the House managers and was not ended until the decision was taken by the votes of the 16th and 26th of May. The eleven articles of impeachment consisted of summaries of all that had been charged against Johnson, except the charge that he had been an accomplice in the murder of Lincoln. The only one which had any real basis was the first, which asserted that he had violated the Tenure of Office Act in trying to remove Stanton. The other articles were merely expansions of the first or were based upon Johnson's opposition to reconstruction or upon his speeches in criticism of Congress. Nothing could be said about his control of the patronage, though this was one of the unwritten charges. J. W. Schuckers, in his life of Chase, says that the radical leaders "felt the vast importance of the presidential patronage; many of them felt, too, that, according to the maxim that to the victors belong the spoils, the Republican party was rightfully entitled to the Federal patronage, and they determined to get possession of it. There was but one method and that was by impeachment and removal of the President."

The leading House managers were Stevens, Butler, Bingham, and Boutwell, all better known as politicians than as lawyers. The President was represented by an abler legal array: Curtis, Evarts, Stanbery, Nelson, and Groesbeck. Jeremiah Black was at first one of the counsel for the President but withdrew under conditions not entirely creditable to himself.

The trial was a one-sided affair. The President's counsel were refused more than six days for the preparation of the case. Chief Justice Chase, who presided over the trial, insisted upon regarding the Senate as a judicial and not a political body, and he accordingly ruled that only legal evidence should be admitted; but the Senate majority preferred to assume that they were settling a political question. Much evidence favorable to the President was excluded, but everything else was admitted. As the trial went on the country began to understand that the impeachment was a mistake. Few people wanted to see Senator Wade made President. The partisan attitude of the Senate majority and the weakness of the case against Johnson had much to do in moderating public opinion, and the timely nomination of General Schofield as Secretary of War after Stanton's resignation reassured those who feared that the army might be placed under some extreme Democrat.

As the time drew near for the decision, every possible pressure was brought by the radicals to induce senators to vote for conviction. To convict the President, thirty-six votes were necessary. There were only twelve Democrats in the Senate, but all were known to be in favor of acquittal. When the test came on the 16th of May, seven Republicans voted with the Democrats for acquittal on the eleventh article. Another vote on the 26th of May, on the first and second articles, showed that conviction was not possible. The radical legislative reaction was thus checked at its highest point and the presidency as a part of the American governmental system was no longer in danger. The seven Republicans had, however, signed their own political death warrants; they were never forgiven by the party leaders.

The presidential campaign was beginning to take shape even before the impeachment trial began. Both the Democrats and the reorganized Republicans were turning with longing toward General Grant as a candidate. Though he had always been a Democrat, nevertheless when Johnson actually called him a liar and a promise breaker Grant went over to the radicals and was nominated for President on May 20, 1868, by the National Union Republican party. Schuyler Colfax was the candidate for Vice President. The Democrats, who could have won with Grant and who under good leadership still had a bare chance to win, nominated Horatio Seymour of New York and Francis P. Blair of Missouri. The former had served as war governor of New York, while the latter was considered an extreme Democrat who believed that the radical reconstruction of the South should be stopped, the troops withdrawn, and the people left to form their own governments. The Democratic platform pronounced itself opposed to the reconstruction policy, but Blair's opposition was too extreme for the North. Seymour, more moderate and a skillful campaigner, made headway in the rehabilitation of the Democratic party. The Republican party declared for radical reconstruction and negro suffrage in the South but held that each Northern State should be allowed to settle the suffrage for itself. It was not a courageous platform, but Grant was popular and carried his party through to success.

The returns showed that in the election Grant had carried twenty-six States with 214 electoral votes, while Seymour had carried only eight States with 80 votes. But an examination of the popular vote, which was 3,000,000 for Grant and 2,700,000 for Seymour, gave the radicals cause for alarm, for it showed that the Democrats had more white votes than the Republicans, whose total included nearly 700,000 blacks. To insure the continuance of the radicals in power, the Fifteenth Amendment was framed and sent out to the States on February 26, 1869. This amendment appeared not only to make safe the negro majorities in the South but also gave the ballot to the negroes in a score of Northern States and thus assured, for a time at least, 900,000 negro voters for the Republican party.

When Johnson's term ended and he gave place to President Grant, four States were still unreconstructed — Virginia, Texas, and Mississippi, in which the reconstruction had failed, and Georgia, which, after accomplishing reconstruction, had again been placed under military rule by Congress. In Virginia, which was too near the capital for such rough work as readmitted Arkansas and Alabama into the Union, the new constitution was so severe in its provisions for disfranchisement that the disgusted district commander would not authorize the expenditure necessary to have it voted on. In Mississippi a similar constitution had failed of adoption, and in Texas the strife of party factions, radical and moderate Republican, had so delayed the framing of the constitution that it had not come to a vote.

The Republican politicians, however, wanted the offices in these States, and Congress by its resolution of February 18, 1869 directed the district commanders to remove all civil officers who could not take the "ironclad" oath and to appoint those who could subscribe to it. An exception, however, was made in favor of the scalawags who had supported reconstruction and whose disabilities had been removed by Congress.

President Grant was anxious to complete the reconstruction and recommended to Congress that the constitutions of Virginia and Mississippi be re-submitted to the people with a separate vote on the disfranchising sections. Congress, now in harmony with the Executive, responded by placing the reconstruction of the three States in the hands of the President, but with the proviso that each State must ratify the Fifteenth Amendment. Grant thereupon fixed a time for voting in each State and directed that in Virginia and Mississippi the disfranchising clauses be submitted separately. As a result, the constitutions were ratified but proscription was voted down. The radicals secured control of Mississippi and Texas, but a conservative combination carried Virginia and thus came near keeping the State out of the Union. Finally, during the early months of 1870 the three States were readmitted.

With respect to Georgia a peculiar condition of affairs existed. In June, 1868, Georgia had been readmitted with the first of the reconstructed

States.   The state legislature at once expelled the twenty-seven negro members, on the ground that the recent legislation and the state constitution gave the negroes the right to vote but not to hold office.   Congress, which had already admitted the Georgia representatives, refused to receive the senators and turned the State back to military control.   In 1869–70 Georgia was again reconstructed after a drastic purging of the Legislature by the military commander, the reseating of the negro members, and the ratification of both the Fourteenth and Fifteenth Amendments.   The State was readmitted to representation in July, 1870, after the failure of a strong effort to extend for two years the carpetbag government of the State.

Upon the last States to pass under the radical yoke heavier conditions were imposed than upon the earlier ones.   Not only were they required to ratify the Fifteenth Amendment, but the "fundamental conditions" embraced, in addition to the prohibition against future change of the suffrage, a requirement that the negroes should never be deprived of school and officeholding rights.

The congressional plan of reconstruction had thus been carried through by able leaders in the face of the opposition of a united white South, nearly half the North, the President, the Supreme Court, and in the beginning a majority of Congress. This success was due to the poor leadership of the conservatives and to the ability and solidarity of the radicals led by Stevens and Sumner. The radicals had a definite program; the moderates had not. The object of the radicals was to secure the supremacy in the South by the aid of the negroes and exclusion of whites. Was this policy politically wise? It was at least temporarily successful. The choice offered by the radicals seemed to lie between military rule for an indefinite period and negro suffrage; and since most Americans found military rule distasteful, they preferred to try negro suffrage. But, after all, negro suffrage had to be supported by military rule, and in the end both failed completely.

CHAPTER VIII

THE UNION LEAGUE OF AMERICA

THE elections of 1867–68 showed that the negroes were well organized under the control of the radical Republican leaders and that their former masters had none of the influence over the blacks in political matters which had been feared by some Northern friends of the negro and had been hoped for by such Southern leaders as Governor Patton and General Hampton. Before 1865 the discipline of slavery, the influence of the master's family, and of the Southern church, had sufficed to control the blacks. But after emancipation they looked to the Federal soldiers and Union officials as the givers of freedom and the guardians of the future.

From the Union soldiers, especially the negro troops, from the Northern teachers, the missionaries and the organizers of negro churches, from the Northern officials and traveling politicians, the negroes learned that their interests were not those of the whites. The attitude of the average white in the South often confirmed this growing estrangement. It was difficult even for the white leaders to explain the riots at Memphis and New Orleans. And those who sincerely wished well for the negro and who desired to control him for the good of both races could not possibly assure him that he was fit for the suffrage. For even Patton and Hampton must tell him that they knew better than he and that he should follow their advice.

The appeal made to freedmen by the Northern leaders was in every way more forceful, because it had behind it the prestige of victory in war and for the future it could promise anything. Until 1867 the principal agency in bringing about the separation of the races had been the Freedmen's Bureau which, with its authority, its courts, its rations, clothes, and its "forty acres and a mule," did effective work in breaking down the influence of the master. But to understand fully the almost absolute control exercised over the blacks in 1867–68 by alien adventurers one must examine the workings of an oath-bound society known as the Union or Loyal League. It was this order, dominated by a few radical whites, which organized, disciplined, and controlled the ignorant negro masses and paralyzed the influence of the conservative whites.

The Union League of America had its origin in Ohio in the fall of 1862, when the outlook for the Union cause was gloomy. The moderate policies of the Lincoln Administration had alienated those in favor of extreme measures; the Confederates had won military successes in the field; the Democrats had made some gains in the elections; the Copperheads[1] were actively opposed to the Washington Government; the Knights of the Golden Circle were organizing to resist the continuance of the war; and the Emancipation Proclamation had chilled the loyalty of many Union men, which was everywhere at a low ebb, especially in the Northern cities. It was to counteract these depressing influences that the Union League movement was begun among those who were associated in the work of the United States Sanitary Commission. Observing the threatening state of public opinion, members of this organization proposed that "loyalty be organized, consolidated and made effective."

The first organization was made by eleven men

[1] See *Abraham Lincoln and the Union*, by Nathaniel W. Stephenson (in *The Chronicles of America*), pp. 156–7, 234–5.

in Cleveland, Ohio, in November, 1862.   The Philadelphia Union League was organized a month
later, and in January, 1863, the New York Union
League followed.   The members were pledged to
uncompromising and unconditional loyalty to the
Union, to complete subordination of political
views to this loyalty, and to the repudiation of
any belief in state rights.   The other large cities followed the example of Philadelphia and New York,
and soon Leagues, connected in a loose federation,
were formed all through the North.   They were
social as well as political in their character and
assumed as their task the stimulation and direction of loyal Union opinion.

As the Union armies proceeded to occupy the
South, the Union League sent its agents among the
disaffected Southern people.   Its agents cared for
negro refugees in the contraband camps and in the
North.   In such work the League coöperated with
the various Freedmen's Aid Societies, the Department of Negro Affairs, and later with the Freedmen's Bureau.   Part of the work of the League
was to distribute campaign literature, and many of
the radical pamphlets on reconstruction and the
negro problem bore the Union League imprint.
The New York League sent out about seventy

thousand copies of various publications, while the Philadelphia League far surpassed this record, circulating within eight years four million five hundred thousand copies of 144 different pamphlets. The literature consisted largely of accounts of "Southern outrages" taken from the reports of Bureau agents and similar sources.

With the close of the Civil War the League did not cease its active interest in things political. It was one of the first organizations to declare for negro suffrage and the disfranchisement of Confederates; it held steadily to this declaration during the four years following the war; and it continued as a sort of bureau in the radical Republican party for the purpose of controlling the negro vote in the South. Its representatives were found in the lobbies of Congress demanding extreme measures, endorsing the reconstruction policies of Congress, and condemning the course of the President. After the first year or two of reconstruction the Leagues in the larger Northern cities began to grow away from the strictly political Union League of America and tended to become mere social clubs for members of the same political belief. The eminently respectable Philadelphia and New York clubs had little in common with the leagues of the Southern and Border States except a general adherence to the radical program.

Even before the end of the war the League was extending its organization into the parts of the Confederacy held by the Federal forces, admitting to membership the army officers and the leading Unionists, though maintaining for the sake of the latter "a discreet secrecy." With the close of the war and the establishment of army posts over the South the League grew rapidly. The civilians who followed the army, the Bureau agents, the missionaries, and the Northern teachers formed one class of membership; and the loyalists of the hill and mountain country, who had become disaffected toward the Confederate administration and had formed such orders as the Heroes of America, the Red String Band, and the Peace Society, formed another class. Soon there were added to these the deserters, a few old line Whigs who intensely disliked the Democrats, and others who decided to cast their lot with the victors. The disaffected politicians of the up-country, who wanted to be cared for in the reconstruction, saw in the organization a means of dislodging from power the political leaders of the low country. It has been estimated that thirty per cent of the white men of the hill and mountain counties of the South joined the Union League in 1865–66. They cared little about the original objects of the order but hoped to make it the nucleus of an anti-Democratic political organization.

But on the admission of negroes into the lodges or councils controlled by Northern men the native white members began to withdraw.   From the beginning the Bureau agents, the teachers, and the preachers had been holding meetings of negroes, to whom they gave advice about the problems of freedom.   Very early these advisers of the blacks grasped the possibilities inherent in their control of the schools, the rationing system, and the churches. By the spring of 1866 the negroes were widely organized under this leadership, and it needed but slight change to convert the negro meetings into local councils of the Union League.[1]   As soon as it seemed likely that Congress would win in its struggle with the President the guardians of the negro planned their campaign for the control

---

[1] Of these teachers of the local blacks, E. L. Godkin, editor of the New York *Nation*, who had supported the reconstruction acts, said: "Worse instructors for men emerging from slavery and coming for the first time face to face with the problems of free life than the radical agitators who have undertaken the political guidance of the blacks it would be hard to meet with."

of the race.   Negro leaders were organized into councils of the League or into Union Republican Clubs. Over the South went the organizers, until by 1868 the last negroes were gathered into the fold.

The native whites did not all desert the Union League when the negroes were brought in. Where the blacks were most numerous the desertion of whites was general, but in the regions where they were few some of the whites remained for several years. The elections of 1868 showed a falling off of the white radical vote from that of 1867, one measure of the extent of loss of whites. From this time forward the order consisted mainly of blacks with enough whites for leaders. In the Black Belt the membership of native whites was discouraged by requiring an oath to the effect that secession was treason. The carpetbagger had found that he could control the negro without the help of the scalawag. The League organization was soon extended and centralized; in every black district there was a Council; for the State there was a Grand Council; and for the United States there was a National Grand Council with headquarters in New York City.

The influence of the League over the negro was

due in large degree to the mysterious secrecy of the meetings, the weird initiation ceremony that made him feel fearfully good from his head to his heels, the imposing ritual, and the songs. The ritual, it is said, was not used in the North; it was probably adopted for the particular benefit of the African. The would-be Leaguer was informed that the emblems of the order were the altar, the Bible, the Declaration of Independence, the Constitution of the United States, the flag of the Union, censer, sword, gavel, ballot box, sickle, shuttle, anvil, and other emblems of industry. He was told to the accompaniment of clanking chains and groans that the objects of the order were to preserve liberty, to perpetuate the Union, to maintain the laws and the Constitution, to secure the ascendancy of American institutions, to protect, defend, and strengthen all loyal men and members of the Union League in all rights of person and property, to demand the elevation of labor, to aid in the education of laboring men, and to teach the duties of American citizenship. This enumeration of the objects of the League sounded well and was impressive. At this point the negro was always willing to take an oath of secrecy, after which he was asked to swear with a solemn oath to support the principles of the Declaration of Independence, to pledge himself to resist all attempts to overthrow the United States, to strive for the maintenance of liberty, the elevation of labor, the education of all people in the duties of citizenship, to practice friendship and charity to all of the order, and to support for election or appointment to office only such men as were supporters of these principles and measures.

The council then sang *Hail, Columbia!* and *The Star Spangled Banner*, after which an official lectured the candidates, saying that though the designs of traitors had been thwarted, there were yet to be secured legislative triumphs and the complete ascendancy of the true principles of popular government, equal liberty, education and elevation of the workmen, and the overthrow at the ballot box of the old oligarchy of political leaders. After prayer by the chaplain, the room was darkened, alcohol on salt flared up with a ghastly light as the "fire of liberty," and the members joined hands in a circle around the candidate, who was made to place one hand on the flag and, with the other raised, swear again to support the government and to elect true Union men to office.   Then placing his hand on a Bible, for the third time he swore to keep his oath, and repeated after the president "the Freedmen's Pledge": "To defend and perpetuate freedom and the Union, I pledge my life, my fortune, and my sacred honor. So help me God!" *John Brown's Body* was then sung, the president charged the members in a long speech concerning the principles of the order, and the marshal instructed the neophyte in the signs. To pass one's self as a Leaguer, the "Four L's" had to be given: (1) with right hand raised to heaven, thumb and third finger touching ends over palm, pronounce "Liberty"; (2) bring the hand down over the shoulder and say "Lincoln"; (3) drop the hand open at the side and say "Loyal"; (4) catch the thumb in the vest or in the waistband and pronounce "League." This ceremony of initiation proved a most effective means of impressing and controlling the negro through his love and fear of secret, mysterious, and midnight mummery. An oath taken in daylight might be forgotten before the next day; not so an oath taken in the dead of night under such impressive circumstances. After passing through the ordeal, the negro usually remained faithful.

In each populous precinct there was at least one council of the League, and always one for blacks.

In each town or city there were two councils, one for the whites, and another, with white officers, for the blacks. The council met once a week, sometimes oftener, nearly always at night, and in a negro church or schoolhouse. Guards, armed with rifles and shotguns, were stationed about the place of meeting in order to keep away intruders. Members of some councils made it a practice to attend the meetings armed as if for battle. In these meetings the negroes listened to inflammatory speeches by the would-be statesmen of the new régime; here they were drilled in a passionate conviction that their interests and those of the Southern whites were eternally at war.

White men who joined the order before the negroes were admitted and who left when the latter became members asserted that the negroes were taught in these meetings that the only way to have peace and plenty, to get "the forty acres and a mule," was to kill some of the leading whites in each community as a warning to others. In North Carolina twenty-eight barns were burned in one county by negroes who believed that Governor Holden, the head of the State League, had ordered it. The council in Tuscumbia, Alabama, received advice from Memphis to use the torch because the blacks were at war with the white race. The advice was taken. Three men went in front of the council as an advance guard, three followed with coal oil and fire, and others guarded the rear. The plan was to burn the whole town, but first one negro and then another insisted on having some white man's house spared because "he is a good man." In the end no residences were burned, and a happy compromise was effected by burning the Female Academy. Three of the leaders were afterwards lynched.

The general belief of the whites was that the ultimate object of the order was to secure political power and thus bring about on a large scale the confiscation of the property of Confederates, and meanwhile to appropriate and destroy the property of their political opponents wherever possible. Chicken houses, pigpens, vegetable gardens, and orchards were visited by members returning from the midnight conclaves. During the presidential campaign of 1868 the North Carolina League sent out circular instructions to the blacks advising them to drill regularly and to join the militia, for if Grant were not elected the negroes would go back to slavery; if he were elected, the negroes were to have farms, mules, and offices.

As soon as possible after the war the negroes had supplied themselves with guns and dogs as badges of freedom. They carried their guns to the League meetings, often marching in military formation, went through the drill there, marched home again along the roads, shouting, firing, and indulging in boasts and threats against persons whom they disliked. Later, military parades in the daytime were much favored. Several hundred negroes would march up and down the streets, abusing whites, and shoving them off the sidewalk or out of the road. But on the whole, there was very little actual violence, though the whites were much alarmed at times. That outrages were comparatively few was due, not to any sensible teachings of the leaders, but to the fundamental good nature of the blacks, who were generally content with mere impudence.

The relations between the races, indeed, continued on the whole to be friendly until 1867–68. For a while, in some localities before the advent of the League, and in others where the Bureau was conducted by native magistrates, the negroes looked to their old masters for guidance and advice; and the latter, for the good of both races, were most eager to retain a moral control over the blacks.

They arranged barbecues and picnics for the negroes, made speeches, gave good advice, and believed that everything promised well. Sometimes the negroes themselves arranged the festival and invited prominent whites, for whom a separate table attended by negro waiters was reserved; and after dinner there followed speeches by both whites and blacks.

With the organization of the League, the negroes grew more reserved, and finally became openly unfriendly to the whites. The League alone, however, was not responsible for this change. The League and the Bureau had to some extent the same personnel, and it is frequently impossible to distinguish clearly between the influence of the two. In many ways the League was simply the political side of the Bureau. The preaching and teaching missionaries were also at work. And apart from the organized influences at work, the poor whites never laid aside their hostility towards the blacks, bond or free.

When the campaigns grew exciting, the discipline of the order was used to prevent the negroes from attending Democratic meetings and hearing Democratic speakers. The leaders even went farther and forbade the attendance of the blacks at political meetings where the speakers were not endorsed by the League. Almost invariably the scalawag disliked the Leaguer, black or white, and as a political teacher often found himself proscribed by the League. At a Republican mass meeting in Alabama a white Republican who wanted to make a speech was shouted down by the negroes because he was "opposed to the Loyal League." He then went to another place to speak but was followed by the crowd, which refused to allow him to say anything. All Republicans in good standing had to join the League and swear that secession was treason — a rather stiff dose for the scalawag. Judge (later Governor) David P. Lewis, of Alabama, was a member for a short while but he soon became disgusted and published a denunciation of the order. Albion W. Tourgée, the author, a radical judge, was the first chief of the League in North Carolina and was succeeded by Governor Holden. In Alabama, Generals Swayne, Spencer, and Warner, all candidates for the United States Senate, hastened to join the order.

As soon as a candidate was nominated by the League, it was the duty of every member to support him actively. Failure to do so resulted in a fine or other more severe punishment, and members who had been expelled were still considered under the control of the officials. The League was, in fact, the machine of the radical party, and all candidates had to be governed by its edicts. As the Montgomery Council declared, the Union League was "the right arm of the Union-Republican party in the United States."

Every negro was *ex colore* a member or under the control of the League. In the opinion of the League, white Democrats were bad enough, but black Democrats were not to be tolerated. It was almost necessary, as a measure of personal safety, for each black to support the radical program. It was possible in some cases for a negro to refrain from taking an active part in political affairs. He might even fail to vote. But it was actually dangerous for a black to be a Democrat; that is, to try to follow his old master in politics. The whites in many cases were forced to advise their few faithful black friends to vote the radical ticket in order to escape mistreatment. Those who showed Democratic leanings were proscribed in negro society and expelled from negro churches; the negro women would not "proshay" (appreciate) a black Democrat. Such a one was sure to find that influence was being brought to bear upon his dusky sweetheart or his wife to cause him to see the error of his ways, and persistent adherence to the white party would result in his losing her. The women were converted to radicalism before the men, and they almost invariably used their influence strongly in behalf of the League. If moral suasion failed to cause the delinquent to see the light, other methods were used. Threats were common and usually sufficed. Fines were levied by the League on recalcitrant members. In case of the more stubborn, a sound beating was effective to bring about a change of heart. The offending party was "bucked and gagged," or he was tied by the thumbs and thrashed. Usually the sufferer was too afraid to complain of the way he was treated.

Some of the methods of the Loyal League were similar to those of the later Ku Klux Klan. Anonymous warnings were sent to obnoxious individuals, houses were burned, notices were posted at night in public places and on the houses of persons who had incurred the hostility of the order. In order to destroy the influence of the whites where kindly relations still existed, an "exodus order" issued through the League directed all members to leave their old homes and obtain work elsewhere. Some of the blacks were loath to comply with this order, but to remonstrances from the whites the usual reply was: "De word done sent to de League. We got to go." For special meetings the negroes were in some regions called together by signal guns. In this way the call for a gathering went out over a county in a few minutes and a few hours later nearly all the members in the county assembled at the appointed place.

Negroes as organizing agents were inclined to go to extremes and for that reason were not so much used. In Bullock County, Alabama, a council of the League was organized under the direction of a negro emissary, who proceeded to assume the government of the community. A list of crimes and punishments was adopted, a court with various officials was established, and during the night the negroes who opposed the new régime were arrested. But the black sheriff and his deputy were in turn arrested by the civil authorities. The negroes then organized for resistance, flocked into the county seat, and threatened to exterminate the whites and take possession of the county. Their agents visited the plantations and forced the laborers to join them by showing orders purporting to be from General Swayne, the commander in the State, giving them the authority to kill all

who resisted them. Swayne, however, sent out
detachments of troops and arrested fifteen of the
ringleaders, and the League government collapsed.

After it was seen that existing political institutions were to be overturned in the process of reconstruction, the white councils of the League and,
to a certain extent, the negro councils were converted into training schools for the leaders of the
new party soon to be formed in the State by act
of Congress. The few whites who were in control
were unwilling to admit more white members to
share in the division of the spoils; terms of admission became more stringent, and, especially
after the passage of the reconstruction acts in
March, 1867, many white applicants were rejected.
The alien element from the North was in control
and as a result, where the blacks were numerous,
the largest plums fell to the carpetbaggers. The
negro leaders — the politicians, preachers, and
teachers — trained in the League acted as subordinates to the whites and were sent out to drum
up the country negroes when elections drew near.
The negroes were given minor positions when
offices were more plentiful than carpetbaggers.
Later, after some complaint, a larger share of the
offices fell to them.

13

The League counted its largest white membership in 1865–66, and after that date it steadily
decreased. The largest negro membership was
recorded in 1867 and 1868. The total membership
was never made known. In North Carolina the
order claimed from seventy-five thousand to one
hundred and twenty-five thousand members; in
States with larger negro populations the membership was probably quite as large. After the election of 1868 only the councils in the towns remained active, many of them transformed into
political clubs, loosely organized under local political leaders. The plantation negro needed less
looking after, and except in the largest towns he
became a kind of visiting member of the council in
the town. The League as a political organization
gradually died out by 1870.[1]

The League had served its purpose. It had
enabled a few outsiders to control the negro by
separating the races politically and it had com-

[1] The Ku Klux Klan had much to do with the decline of the organization. The League as the ally and successor of the Freedmen's
Bureau was one of the causes of the Ku Klux movement, because it
helped to create the conditions which made such a movement inevitable. As early as 1870 the radical leaders missed the support
formerly given by the League, and an urgent appeal was sent out
all over the South from headquarters in New York advocating its
reëstablishment to assist in carrying the elections of 1870.

pelled the negroes to vote as radicals for several years, when without its influence they would either not have voted at all or would have voted as Democrats along with their former masters. The order was necessary to the existence of the radical party in the Black Belt. No ordinary political organization could have welded the blacks into a solid party. The Freedmen's Bureau, which had much influence over the negroes, was too weak in numbers to control the negroes in politics. The League finally absorbed the personnel of the Bureau and turned its prestige and its organization to political advantage.

CHAPTER IX

CHURCH AND SCHOOL

RECONSTRUCTION in the State was closely related to reconstruction in the churches and the schools. Here also were to be found the same hostile elements: negro and white, Unionist and Confederate, victor and vanquished. The church was at that time an important institution in the South, more so than in the North, and in both sections more important than it is today. It was inevitable, therefore, that ecclesiastical reconstruction should give rise to bitter feelings.

Something should be said of conditions in the churches when the Federal armies occupied the land. The Southern organizations had lost many ministers and many of their members, and frequently their buildings were used as hospitals or had been destroyed. Their administration was disorganized and their treasuries were empty. The Unionists, scattered here and there but numerous in the mountain districts, no longer wished to attend the Southern churches.

The military censorship in church matters, which continued for a year in some districts, was irritating, especially in the Border States and in the Union districts where Northern preachers installed by the army were endeavoring to remain against the will of the people. Mobs sometimes drove them out; others were left to preach to empty houses or to a few Unionists and officers, while the congregation withdrew to build a new church. The problems of negro membership in the white churches and of the future relations of the Northern and Southern denominations were pressing for settlement.

All Northern organizations acted in 1865 upon the assumption that a reunion of the churches must take place and that the divisions existing before the war should not be continued, since slavery, the cause of the division, had been destroyed. But they insisted that the reunion must take place upon terms named by the "loyal" churches, that the negroes must also come under "loyal" religious direction, and that tests must be applied to the Confederate sinners asking for admission, in order that the enormity of their crimes should be made plain to them. But this policy did not succeed. The Confederates objected to being treated as "rebels and traitors" and to "sitting upon stools of repentance" before they should be received again into the fold.

Only two denominations were reunited — the Methodist Protestant, the northern section of which came over to the southern, and the Protestant Episcopal, in which moderate counsels prevailed and into which Southerners were welcomed back. The Southern Baptists maintained their separate existence and reorganized the Southern Baptist Convention, to which came many of the Baptist associations in the Border States; the Catholics did not divide before 1861 and therefore had no reconstruction problems to solve; and the smaller denominations maintained the organizations which they had before 1861. A Unionist preacher testified before the Joint Committee on Reconstruction that even the Southern Quakers "are about as decided in regard to the respectability of secession as any other class of people."

Two other great Southern churches, the Presbyterian and the Methodist Episcopal, grew stronger after the Civil War. The tendency toward reunion of the Presbyterians was checked when one Northern branch declared as "a condition precedent to the admission of southern applicants that these confess as sinful all opinions before held in regard to slavery, nullification, rebellion and slavery, and stigmatize secession as a crime and the withdrawal of the southern churches as a schism." Another Northern group declared that Southern ministers must be placed on probation and must either prove their loyalty or profess repentance for disloyalty and repudiate their former opinions. As a result several Presbyterian bodies in the South joined in a strong union, to which also adhered the synods of several Border States.

The Methodist Episcopal Church, South, was confronted with conditions similar to those which prevented the reunion of the Presbyterians. The Northern church, according to the declaration of its authorities, also came down to divide the spoils and to "disintegrate and absorb" the "schismatic" Southern churches. Already many Southern pulpits were filled with Northern Methodist ministers placed there under military protection; and when they finally realized that reunion was not possible, these Methodist worthies resolved to occupy the late Confederacy as a mission field and to organize congregations of blacks and whites who were "not tainted with treason." Bishops and clergymen charged with this work carried it on vigorously for a few years in close connection with political reconstruction.

The activities of the Northern Methodists stimulated the Southern Methodists to a quick reorganization. The surviving bishops met in August, 1865, and bound together their shaken church. In reply to suggestions of reunion they asserted that the Northern Methodists had become "incurably radical," were too much involved in politics, and, further, that they had, without right, seized and were still holding Southern church buildings. They objected also to the way the Northern church referred to the Southerners as "schismatics" and to the Southern church as one built on slavery and therefore, now that slavery was gone, to be reconstructed. The bishops warned their people against the missionary efforts of the Northern brethren and against the attempts to "disintegrate and absorb" Methodism in the South. Within five years after the war the Methodist Episcopal Church, South, was greatly increased in numbers by the accession of conferences in Maryland, Kentucky, Virginia, Missouri, and even from above the Ohio, while the Northern

Methodist Church was able to organize only a few
white congregations outside of the stronger Unionist districts, but continued to labor in the South
as a missionary field.[1]

But if the large Southern churches held their
white membership and even gained in numbers and
territory, they fought a losing fight to retain their
black members. It was assumed by Northern
ecclesiastics that whether a reunion of whites took
place or not, the negroes would receive spiritual
guidance from the North. This was necessary,
they said, because the Southern whites were ignorant and impoverished and because "the state of
mind among even the best classes of Southern

[1] The church situation after the war was well described in 1866 by
an editorial writer in the *Nation* who pointed out that the Northern
churches thought the South determined to make the religious division
permanent, though "slavery no longer furnishes a pretext for separation." "Too much pains were taken to bring about an ecclesiastical
reunion, and irritating offers of reconciliation are made by the Northern churches, all based on the assumption that the South has not only
sinned, but sinned knowingly, in slavery and in war. We expect them
to be penitent and to gladly accept our offers of forgiveness. But the
Southern people look upon a 'loyal' missionary as a political emissary,
and 'loyal' men do not at present possess the necessary qualifications
for evangelizing the Southerners or softening their hearts, and are
sure not to succeed in doing so. We look upon their defeat as retribu-
tion and expect them to do the same. It will do no good if we tell the
Southerner that 'we will forgive them if they will confess that they
are criminals, offer to pray with them, preach with them, and labor
with them over their hideous sins.'"

whites rendered them incapable . . . of doing justice to the people whom they had so long persistently wronged." Further, it was also necessary for political reasons to remove the negroes from Southern religious control.

For obvious reasons, however, the Southern churches wanted to hold their negro members. They declared themselves in favor of negro education and of better organized religious work among the blacks, and made every sort of accommodation to hold them. The Baptists organized separate congregations, with white or black pastors as desired, and associations of black churches. In 1866 the Methodist General Conference authorized separate congregations, quarterly conferences, annual conferences, even a separate jurisdiction, with negro preachers, presiding elders, and bishops — but all to no avail. Every Northern political, religious, or military agency in the South worked for separation, and negro preachers were not long in seeing the greater advantages which they would have in independent churches.

Much of the separate organization was accomplished in mutual good will, particularly in the Baptist ranks. The Reverend I. T. Tichenor, a prominent Baptist minister, has described the process as it took place in the First Baptist Church in Montgomery. The church had nine hundred members, of whom six hundred were black. The negroes received a regular organization of their own under the supervision of the white pastors. When a separation of the two bodies was later deemed desirable, it was inaugurated by a conference of the negroes which passed a resolution couched in the kindliest terms, suggesting the wisdom of the division, and asking the concurrence of the white church in such action. The white church cordially approved the movement, and the two bodies united in erecting a suitable house of worship for the negroes. Until the new church was completed, both congregations continued to occupy jointly the old house of worship. The new house was paid for in large measure by the white members of the church and by individuals in the community. As soon as it was completed the colored church moved into it with its pastor, board of deacons, committees of all sorts, and the whole machinery of church life went into action without a jar. Similar accommodations occurred in all the States of the South.

The Methodists lost the greater part of their negro membership to two organizations which came down from the North in 1865 — the African Methodist Episcopal Church and the African Methodist Episcopal Church, Zion. Large numbers also went over to the Northern Methodist Church. After losing nearly three hundred thousand members, the Southern Methodists came to the conclusion that the remaining seventy-eight thousand negroes would be more comfortable in a separate organization and therefore began in 1866 the Colored Methodist Episcopal Church, with bishops, conferences, and all the accompaniments of the parent Methodist Church, which continued to give friendly aid but exercised no control. For many years the Colored Methodist Church was under fire from the other negro denominations, who called it the "rebel," the "Democratic," the "old slavery" church.

The negro members of the Cumberland Presbyterians were similarly set off into a small African organization. The Southern Presbyterians and the Episcopalians established separate congregations and missions under white supervision but sanctioned no independent negro organization. Consequently the negroes soon deserted these churches and went with their own kind.

Resentment at the methods employed by the

Northern religious carpetbaggers was strong among
the Southern whites. "Emissaries of Christ and
the radical party" they were called by one Alabama leader. Governor Lindsay of the same State
asserted that the Northern missionaries caused
race hatred by teaching the negroes to regard the
whites as their natural enemies, who, if possible,
would put them back in slavery. Others were
charged with teaching that to be on the safe side,
the blacks should get into a Northern church, and
that "Christ died for negroes and Yankees, not
for rebels."

The scalawags, also, developed a dislike of the
Northern church work among the negroes and it
was impossible to organize mixed congregations.
Of the Reverend A. S. Lakin, a well-known agent
of the Northern Methodist Church in Alabama,
Nicholas Davis, a North Alabama Unionist and
scalawag, said to the Ku Klux Committee: "The
character of his [Lakin's] speech was this: to teach
the negroes that every man that was born and
raised in the Southern country was their enemy,
that there was no use trusting them, no matter
what they said — if they said they were for the
Union or anything else. 'No use talking, they are
your enemies.' And he made a pretty good speech,

too; awful; a hell of a one; . . . inflammatory and game, too. . . . It was enough to provoke the devil. Did all the mischief he could . . . I tell you, that old fellow is a hell of an old rascal."

For a time the white churches were annoyed by intrusions of strange blacks set on by those who were bent on separating the races. Frequently there were feuds in white or black congregations over the question of joining some Northern body. Disputes over church property also arose and continued for years. Lakin, referred to above, was charged with "stealing" negro congregations and uniting them with the Cincinnati Conference without their knowledge. The negroes were urged to demand title to all buildings formerly used for negro worship, and the Constitutional Convention of Alabama in 1867 directed that such property must be turned over to them when claimed.

The agents of the Northern churches were not greatly different from other carpetbaggers and adventurers taking advantage of the general confusion to seize a little power. Many were unscrupulous; others, sincere and honest but narrow, bigoted, and intolerant, filled with distrust of the Southern whites and with corresponding confidence in the blacks and in themselves. The missionary and church publications were quite as severe on the Southern people as any radical Congressman. The publications of the Freedmen's Aid Society furnish illustrations of the feelings and views of those engaged in the Southern work. They in turn were made to feel the effects of a merciless social proscription. For this some of them cared not at all, while others or their families felt it keenly. One woman missionary wrote that she was delighted when a Southern white would speak to her. A preacher in Virginia declared that "the females, those especially whose pride has been humbled, are more intense in their bitterness and endeavor to keep up a social ostracism against Union and Northern people." The Ku Klux raids were directed against preachers and congregations whose conduct was disagreeable to the whites. Lakin asserted that while he was conducting a great revival meeting among the hills of northern Alabama, Governor Smith and other prominent and sinful scalawag politicians were there "under conviction" and about to become converted. But in came the Klan and the congregation scattered. Smith and the others were so angry and frightened that their good feelings were dissipated, and the devil reëntered them, so that Lakin said he was never able to "get a hold on them" again. For the souls lost that night he held the Klan responsible. Lakin told several marvelous stories of his hairbreadth escapes from death by assassination which, if true, would be enough to ruin the reputation of northern Alabama men for marksmanship.

The reconstruction ended with conditions in the churches similar to those in politics: the races were separated and unfriendly; Northern and Southern church organizations were divided; and between them, especially in the border and mountain districts, there existed factional quarrels of a political origin, for every Northern Methodist was a Republican and every Southern Methodist was a Democrat.

The schools of the South, like the churches and political institutions, were thrown into the melting pot of reconstruction. The spirit in which the work was begun may be judged from the tone of the addresses made at a meeting of the National Teachers Association in 1865. The president, S. S. Greene, declared that "the old slave States are to be the new missionary ground for the national school teacher." Francis Wayland, the former president of Brown University, remarked that "it has been a war of education and patriotism against ignorance and barbarism." President Hill of Harvard spoke of the "new work of spreading knowledge and intellectual culture over the regions that sat in darkness." Other speakers asserted that the leading Southern whites were as much opposed to free schools as to free governments and "we must treat them as western farmers do the stumps in their clearings, work around them and let them rot out"; that the majority of the whites were more ignorant than the slaves; and that the negro must be educated and strengthened against "the wiles, the guile, and hate of his baffled masters and their minions." The New England Freedmen's Aid Society considered it necessary to educate the negro "as a counteracting influence against the evil councils and designs of the white freemen."

The tasks that confronted the Southern States in 1865–67 were two: first, to restore the shattered school systems of the whites; and second, to arrange for the education of the negroes. Education of the negro slave had been looked upon as dangerous and had been generally forbidden. A small number of negroes could read and write, but there were at the close of the war no schools for the children.   Before 1861 each State had developed at least the outlines of a school system. Though hindered in development by the sparseness of the population and by the prevalence in some districts of the Virginia doctrine that free schools were only for the poor, public schools were nevertheless in existence in 1861.   Academies and colleges, however, were thronged with students.   When the war ended, the public schools were disorganized, and the private academies and the colleges were closed.   Teachers and students had been dispersed; buildings had been burned or used for hospitals and laboratories; and public libraries had virtually disappeared.

The colleges made efforts to open in the fall of 1865.   Only one student presented himself at the University of Alabama for matriculation; but before June, 1866, the stronger colleges were again in operation.   The public or semi-public schools for the whites also opened in the fall.   In the cities where Federal military authorities had brought about the employment of Northern teachers, there was some friction.   In New Orleans, for example, the teachers required the children to sing Northern songs and patriotic airs.   When the Confederates were restored to power these teachers were dismissed.

The movement toward negro education was general throughout the South. Among the blacks themselves there was an intense desire to learn. They wished to read the Bible, to be preachers, to be as the old master and not have to work. Day and night and Sunday they crowded the schools. According to an observer,[1] "not only are individuals seen at study, and under the most untoward circumstances, but in very many places I have found what I will call 'native schools,' often rude and very imperfect, but there they are, a group, perhaps, of all ages, trying to learn. Some young man, some woman, or old preacher, in cellar, or shed, or corner of a negro meeting-house, with the alphabet in hand, or a town spelling-book, is their teacher. All are full of enthusiasm with the new knowledge the book is imparting to them."

Not only did the negroes want schooling, but both the North and the South proposed to give it to them. Neither side was actuated entirely by altruistic motives. A Hampton Institute teacher in later days remarked: "When the combat was over and the Yankee school-ma'ams followed in the train of the northern armies, the business of

[1] J. W. Alvord, Superintendent of Schools for the Freedmen's Bureau, 1866.

educating the negroes was a continuation of hostilities against the vanquished and was so regarded to
a considerable extent on both sides."

The Southern churches, through their bishops
and clergy, the newspapers, and prominent individuals such as J. L. M. Curry, John B. Gordon, J. L.
Orr, Governors Brown, Moore, and Patton, came
out in favor of negro education. Of this movement General Swayne said: "Quite early . . .
the several religious denominations took strong
ground in favor of the education of the freedmen.
The principal argument was an appeal to sectional
and sectarian prejudice, lest, the work being inevitable, the influence which must come from it be
realized by others; but it is believed that this was
but the shield and weapon which men of unselfish
principle found necessary at first."   The newspapers took the attitude that the Southern whites
should teach the negroes because it was their duty,
because it was good policy, and because if they did
not do so some one else would.   The *Advertiser* of
Montgomery stated that education was a danger
in slavery times but that under freedom ignorance
became a danger.   For a time there were numerous schools taught by crippled Confederates and
by Southern women.

But the education of the negro, like his religious training, was taken from the control of the Southern white and was placed under the direction of the Northern teachers and missionaries who swarmed into the country under the fostering care of the Freedmen's Bureau, the Northern churches, and the various Freedmen's Aid Societies. In three years the Bureau spent six million dollars on negro schools and everywhere it exercised supervision over them. The teachers pursued a policy akin to that of the religious leaders. One Southerner likened them to the "plagues of Egypt," another described them as "saints, fools, incendiaries, fakirs, and plain business men and women." A Southern woman remarked that "their spirit was often high and noble so far as the black man's elevation was concerned, but toward the white it was bitter, judicial, and unrelenting." The Northern teachers were charged with ignorance of social conditions, with fraternizing with the blacks, and with teaching them that the Southerners were traitors, "murderers of Lincoln," who had been cruel taskmasters and who now wanted to restore servitude.

The reaction against negro education, which began to show itself before reconstruction was inaugurated, found expression in the view of most whites that "schooling ruins a negro." A more intelligent opinion was that of J. L. M. Curry, a lifelong advocate of negro education:

It is not just to condemn the negro for the education which he received in the early years after the war. That was the period of reconstruction, the saturnalia of misgovernment, the greatest possible hindrance to the progress of the freedmen. . . . The education was unsettling, demoralizing, [and it] pandered to a wild frenzy for schooling as a quick method of reversing social and political conditions. Nothing could have been better devised for deluding the poor negro and making him the tool, the slave of corrupt taskmasters. Education is a natural consequence of citizenship and enfranchisement . . . of freedom and humanity. But with deliberate purpose to subject the Southern States to negro domination, and secure the States permanently for partisan ends, the education adopted was contrary to commonsense, to human experience, to all noble purposes. The curriculum was for a people in the highest degree of civilization; the aptitude and capabilities and needs of the negro were wholly disregarded. Especial stress was laid on classics and liberal culture to bring the race *per saltum* to the same plane with their former masters, and realize the theory of social and political equality. A race more highly civilized, with best heredities and environments, could not have been coddled with more disregard of all the teachings of human history and the necessities of the race. Colleges and universities, established and conducted by the Freedmen's Bureau and Northern churches and societies, sprang up like mushrooms, and the teachers, ignorant, fanatical, without self-poise, proceeded to make all possible mischief. It is irrational, cruel, to hold the negro, under such strange conditions, responsible for all the ill consequences of bad education, unwise teachers, reconstruction villanies, and partisan schemes.[1]

Education was to be looked upon as a handmaid to a thorough reconstruction, and its general character and aim were determined by the Northern teachers. Each convention framed a more or less complicated school system and undertook to provide for its support. The negroes in the conventions were anxious for free schools; the conservatives were willing; but the carpetbaggers and a few mulatto leaders insisted in several States upon mixed schools. Only in Louisiana and South Carolina did the constitutions actually forbid separate schools; in Mississippi, Florida, Alabama, and Arkansas the question was left open, to the embarrassment of the whites. Generally the blacks showed no desire for mixed schools unless urged to it by the carpetbaggers. In the South Carolina convention a mulatto thus argued in favor of mixed schools: "The gentleman from Newberry said he was afraid we were taking a wrong

[1] Quoted in *Proceedings* of the Montgomery Conference on Race Problems (1900), p. 128.

course to remove these prejudices. The most natural method to effect this object would be to allow children when five or six years of age to mingle in schools together and associate generally. Under such training, prejudice must eventually die out; but if we postpone it until they become men and women, prejudice will be so established that no mortal can obliterate it. This, I think, is a sufficient reply to the argument of the gentleman."

The state systems were top-heavy with administrative machinery and were officered by incompetent and corrupt officials. Such men as Cloud in Alabama, Cardozo in Mississippi, Conway in Louisiana, and Jillson in South Carolina are fair samples of them. Much of the personnel was taken over from the Bureau teaching force. The school officials were no better than the other officeholders.

The first result of the attempt to use the schools as an instrument of reconstruction ended in the ruin of several state universities. The faculties of the Universities of North Carolina, Mississippi, and Alabama were made radical and the institutions thereupon declined to nothing. The negroes, unable to control the faculty of the University of South Carolina, forced negro students in and thus got possession. In Louisiana the radical Legislature cut off all funds because the university would not admit negroes. The establishment of the land grant colleges was an occasion for corruption and embezzlement.

The common schools were used for radical ends. The funds set aside for them by the state constitutions or appropriated by the legislatures for these schools seldom reached their destination without being lessened by embezzlement or by plain stealing. Frequently the auditor, or the treasurer, or even the Legislature diverted the school funds to other purposes. Suffice it to say that all of the reconstruction systems broke down financially after a brief existence.

The mixed school provisions in Louisiana and South Carolina and the uncertainty of the educational situation in other States caused white children to stay away from the public schools. For several years the negroes were better provided than the whites, having for themselves both all the public schools and also those supported by private benevolence. In Mississippi, Louisiana, and South Carolina the whites could get no money for schoolhouses, while large sums were spent on negro schools. The Peabody Board, then recently inaugurated,[1] refused to coöperate with school officials in the mixed school States and, when criticized, replied: "It is well known that we are helping the white children of Louisiana as being the more destitute from the fact of their unwillingness to attend mixed schools."

As was to be expected the whites criticized the attitude of the school officials, disapproved of the attempts made in the schools to teach the children radical ideas, and objected to the contents of the history texts and the "Freedmen's Readers." A white school board in Mississippi, by advertising for a Democratic teacher for a negro school, drew the fire of a radical editor who inquired: "What is the motive by which this call for a 'competent Democratic teacher' is prompted? The most damning that has ever moved the heart of man. It is to use the vote and action of a human being as a means by which to enslave him. The treachery and villainy of these rebels stands without parallel in the history of men."

A negro politician has left this account of a radical recitation in a Florida negro school:

[1] To administer the fund bequeathed by George Peabody of Massachusetts to promote education in the Southern States. See *The New South*, by Holland Thompson (in *The Chronicles of America*).

After finishing the arithmetic lesson they must next go through the catechism:

"Who is the 'Publican Government of the State of Florida?" *Answer:* "Governor Starns."

"Who made him Governor?" *Answer:* "The colored people."

"Who is trying to get him out of his seat?" *Answer:* "The Democrats, Conover, and some white and black Liberal Republicans."

"What should the colored people do with the men who is trying to get Governor Starns out of his seat?" *Answer:* "They should kill them." . . .

This was done that the patrons, some of whom could not read, would be impressed by the expressions of their children, and would be ready to put any one to death who would come out into the country and say anything against Governor Starns.

The native white teachers soon dropped out of negro schools, and those from the North met with the same social persecution as the white church workers. The White League and Ku Klux Klan drove off obnoxious teachers, whipped some, burned negro schoolhouses, and in various other ways manifested the reaction which was rousing the whites against negro schools.

The several agencies working for negro education gave some training to hundreds of thousands of blacks, but the whites asserted that, like the church work, it was based on a wrong spirit and resulted in evil as well as in good. Free schools failed in reconstruction because of the dishonesty or incompetence of the authorities and because of the unsettled race question. It was not until the turn of the century that the white schools were again as good as they had been before 1861. After the reconstruction native whites as teachers of negro schools were impossible in most places. The hostile feelings of the whites resulted and still result in a limitation of negro schools. The best thing for negro schools that came out of reconstruction was Armstrong's Hampton Institute program, which, however, was quite opposed to the spirit of reconstruction education.

CHAPTER X

CARPETBAG AND NEGRO RULE

THE Southern States reconstructed by Congress were subject for periods of varying length to governments designed by radical Northerners and imposed by elements thrown to the surface in the upheaval of Southern society. Georgia, Virginia, and North Carolina each had a brief experience with these governments; other States escaped after four or five years, while Louisiana, South Carolina, and Florida were not delivered from this domination until 1876. The States which contained large numbers of negroes had, on the whole, the worst experience. Here the officials were ignorant or corrupt, frauds upon the public were the rule, not the exception, and all of the reconstruction governments were so conducted that they could secure no support from the respectable elements of the electorate.

The fundamental cause of the failure of these

governments was the character of the new ruling class. Every State, except perhaps Virginia, was under the control of a few able leaders from the North generally called carpetbaggers and of a few native white radicals contemptuously designated scalawags. These were kept in power by negro voters, to some seven hundred thousand of whom the ballot had been given by the reconstruction acts. The adoption of the Fifteenth Amendment in March, 1870, brought the total in the former slave States to 931,000, with about seventy-five thousand more negroes in the North. The negro voters were most numerous, comparatively, in Louisiana, Mississippi, South Carolina, Alabama, and Georgia. There were a few thousand carpetbaggers in each State, with, at first, a much larger number of scalawags. The latter, who were former Unionists, former Whigs, Confederate deserters, and a few unscrupulous politicians, were most numerous in Virginia, North Carolina, Texas, Arkansas, and Tennessee. The better class, however, rapidly left the radical party as the character of the new régime became evident, taking with them whatever claims the party had to respectability, education, political experience, and property.

The conservatives, hopelessly reduced by the

operation of disfranchising laws, were at first not well organized, nor were they at any time as well led as in antebellum days. In 1868 about one hundred thousand of them were forbidden to vote and about two hundred thousand were disqualified from holding office. The abstention policy of 1867–68 resulted in an almost complete withdrawal of the influence of the conservatives for the two years, 1868–70. As a class they were regarded by the dominant party in State and nation as dangerous and untrustworthy and were persecuted in such irritating ways that many became indifferent to the appeals of civil duty. They formed a solid but almost despairing opposition in the black districts of Mississippi, Louisiana, Alabama, and South Carolina. For the leaders the price of amnesty was conversion to radicalism, but this price few would pay.

The new state governments possessed certain characteristics in common. Since only a small number of able men were available for office, full powers of administration, including appointment and removal, were concentrated in the hands of the governor. He exercised a wide control over public funds and had authority to organize and command militia and constabulary and to call for Federal troops. The numerous administrative boards worked with the sole object of keeping their party in power. Officers were several times as numerous as under the old régime, and all of them received higher salaries and larger contingent fees. The moral support behind the government was that of President Grant and the United States army, not that of a free and devoted people.

Of the twenty men who served as governors eight were scalawags and twelve were carpetbaggers — men who were abler than the scalawags and who had much more than an equal share of the spoils. The scalawags, such as Brownlow of Tennessee, Smith of Alabama, and Holden of North Carolina, were usually honest but narrow, vindictive men, filled with fear and hate of the conservative whites. Of the carpetbaggers half were personally honest, but all were unscrupulous in politics. Some were flagrantly dishonest. Governor Moses of South Carolina was several times bribed and at one time, according to his own statement, received $15,000 for his vote as speaker of the House of Representatives. Governor Stearns of Florida was charged with stealing government supplies from the negroes; and it was notorious that Warmoth and Kellogg of Louisiana, each of whom served only

one term, retired with large fortunes.   Warmoth,
indeed, went so far as to declare: "Corruption is
the fashion.   I do not pretend to be honest, but
only as honest as anybody in politics."

The judiciary was no better than the executive.
The chief justice of Louisiana was convicted of
fraud.   A supreme court judge of South Carolina
offered his decisions for sale, and Whipper and
Moses, both notorious thieves, were elected judges
by the South Carolina Legislature.   In Alabama
there were many illiterate magistrates, among
them the city judge of Selma, who in April, 1865,
was still living as a slave.   Governor Chamberlain,
a radical, asserted that there were two hundred
trial judges in South Carolina who could not read.

Other officers were of the same stripe.   Les-
lie, a South Carolina carpetbagger, declared that
"South Carolina has no right to be a State unless
she can support her statesmen," and he proceeded
to live up to this principle.   The manager of the
state railroad of Georgia, when asked how he had
been able to accumulate twenty or thirty thousand
dollars on a two or three thousand dollar salary,
replied, "By the exercise of the most rigid economy."   A North Carolina negro legislator was
found on one occasion chuckling as he counted

some money. "What are you laughing at, Uncle?" he was asked. "Well, boss, I'se been sold 'leben times in my life and dis is de fust time I eber got de money." Godkin, in the *Nation*, said that the Georgia officials were "probably as bad a lot of political tricksters and adventurers as ever got together in one place." This description will fit equally well the white officials of all the reconstructed States. Many of the negroes who attained public office showed themselves apt pupils of their carpetbag masters but were seldom permitted to appropriate a large share of the plunder. In Florida the negro members of the Legislature, thinking that they should have a part of the bribe and loot money which their carpetbag masters were said to be receiving, went so far as to appoint what was known as a "smelling committee" to locate the good things and secure a share.

From 1868 to 1870 the legislatures of seven States were overwhelmingly radical and in several the radical majority held control for four, six, or eight years. Negroes were most numerous in the legislatures of Louisiana, South Carolina, and Mississippi, and everywhere the votes of these men were for sale. In Alabama and Louisiana negro legislators had a fixed price for their votes: for example, six hundred dollars would buy a senator in Louisiana. In South Carolina, negro government appeared at its worst. A vivid description of the Legislature of this State in which the negroes largely outnumbered the whites is given by James S. Pike, a Republican journalist[1]:

In the place of this old aristocratic society stands the rude form of the most ignorant democracy that mankind ever saw, invested with the functions of government. It is the dregs of the population habilitated in the robes of their intelligent predecessors, and asserting over them the rule of ignorance and corruption. . . . It is barbarism overwhelming civilization by physical force. It is the slave rioting in the halls of his master, and putting that master under his feet. And, though it is done without malice and without vengeance, it is nevertheless none the less completely and absolutely done. . . . We will enter the House of Representatives. Here sit one hundred and twenty-four members. Of these, twenty-three are white men, representing the remains of the old civilization. These are good-looking, substantial citizens. They are men of weight and standing in the communities they represent. They are all from the hill country. The frosts of sixty and seventy winters whiten the heads of some among them. There they sit, grim and silent. They feel themselves to be but loose stones, thrown in to partially obstruct a current they are powerless to resist. . . .
This dense negro crowd . . . do the debating, the

[1] Pike, *The Prostrate State*, pp. 12 ff.

squabbling, the lawmaking, and create all the clamor
and disorder of the body.   These twenty-three white
men are but the observers, the enforced auditors of the
dull and clumsy imitation of a deliberative body, whose
appearance in their present capacity is at once a wonder
and a shame to modern civilization. . . .   The Speaker is
black, the Clerk is black, the doorkeepers are black, the
little pages are black, the chairman of the Ways and
Means is black, and the chaplain is coal black.   At some
of the desks sit colored men whose types it would be
hard to find outside of Congo; whose costumes, visages,
attitudes, and expression, only befit the forecastle of a
buccaneer.   It must be remembered, also, that these
men, with not more than a half dozen exceptions, have
been themselves slaves, and that their ancestors were
slaves for generations. . . .

But the old stagers admit that the colored brethren
have a wonderful aptness at legislative proceedings.
They are "quick as lightning" at detecting points of
order, and they certainly make incessant and extraordinary use of their knowledge.   No one is allowed to talk
five minutes without interruption, and one interruption
is a signal for another and another, until the original
speaker is smothered under an avalanche of them.   Forty
questions of privilege will be raised in a day.   At times,
nothing goes on but alternating questions of order and of
privilege.   The inefficient colored friend who sits in the
Speaker's chair cannot suppress this extraordinary element of the debate.   Some of the blackest members
exhibit a pertinacity of intrusion in raising these points
of order and questions of privilege that few white men
can equal.   Their struggles to get the floor, their bel-
lowings and physical contortions, baffle description.

The Speaker's hammer plays a perpetual tattoo to no purpose. The talking and the interruptions from all quarters go on with the utmost license. Everyone esteems himself as good as his neighbor, and puts in his oar, apparently as often for love of riot and confusion as for anything else. . . . The Speaker orders a member whom he has discovered to be particularly unruly to take his seat. The member obeys, and with the same motion that he sits down, throws his feet on to his desk, hiding himself from the Speaker by the soles of his boots. . . . After a few experiences of this sort, the Speaker threatens, in a laugh, to call the "gemman" to order. This is considered a capital joke, and a guffaw follows. The laugh goes round and then the peanuts are cracked and munched faster than ever; one hand being employed in fortifying the inner man with this nutriment of universal use, while the other enforces the views of the orator. This laughing propensity of the sable crowd is a great cause of disorder. They laugh as hens cackle — one begins and all follow.

But underneath all this shocking burlesque upon legislative proceedings, we must not forget that there is something very real to this uncouth and untutored multitude. It is not all sham, nor all burlesque. They have a genuine interest and a genuine earnestness in the business of the assembly which we are bound to recognize and respect. . . . They have an earnest purpose, born of conviction that their position and condition are not fully assured, which lends a sort of dignity to their proceedings. The barbarous, animated jargon in which they so often indulge is on occasion seen to be so transparently sincere and weighty in their own minds that sympathy supplants disgust. The whole thing is a wonderful novelty

to them as well as to observers. Seven years ago these
men were raising corn and cotton under the whip of the
overseer. Today they are raising points of order and
questions of privilege. They find they can raise one as
well as the other. They prefer the latter. It is easier
and better paid. Then, it is the evidence of an accomplished result. It means escape and defense from old
oppressors. It means liberty. It means the destruction of prison-walls only too real to them. It is the sun-
shine of their lives. It is their day of jubilee. It is
their long-promised vision of the Lord God Almighty.

The congressional delegations were as radical as
the state governments. During the first two years
there were no Democratic senators from the reconstructed States and only two Democratic representatives, as against sixty-four radical senators and
representatives. At the end of four years the Democrats numbered fifteen against seventy radicals.
A negro succeeded Jefferson Davis in the Senate,
and in all the race sent two senators and thirteen
representatives to Congress, but though several
were of high character and fair ability, they exercised practically no influence. The Southern delegations had no part in shaping policies but merely
voted as they were told by the radical leaders.

The effect of dishonest government was soon
seen in extravagant expenditures, heavier taxes,

increase of the bonded debt, and depression of property values. It was to be expected that after the ruin wrought by war and the admission of the negro to civil rights, the expenses of government would be greater. But only lack of honesty will account for the extraordinary expenses of the reconstruction governments. In Alabama and Florida the running expenses of the state government increased two hundred per cent, in Louisiana five hundred per cent, and in Arkansas fifteen hundred per cent — all this in addition to bond issues. In South Carolina the one item of public printing, which from 1790 to 1868 cost $609,000, amounted in the years 1868–1876 to $1,326,589.

Corrupt state officials had two ways of getting money — by taxation and by the sale of bonds. Taxes were everywhere multiplied. The state tax rate in Alabama was increased four hundred per cent, in Louisiana eight hundred per cent, and in Mississippi, which could issue no bonds, fourteen hundred per cent. City and county taxes, where carpetbaggers were in control, increased in the same way. Thousands of small proprietors could not meet their taxes, and in Mississippi alone the land sold for unpaid taxes amounted to six million acres, an area as large as Massachusetts and

Rhode Island together.   Nordhoff[1] speaks of seeing Louisiana newspapers of which three-fourths were taken up by notices of tax sales. In protest against extravagant and corrupt expenditures, taxpayers' conventions were held in every State, but without effect.

Even the increased taxation, however, did not produce enough to support the new governments, which now had recourse to the sale of state and local bonds.   In this way Governor Holden's Administration managed in two years to increase the public debt of North Carolina from $16,000,000 to $32,000,000.   The state debt of South Carolina rose from $7,000,000 to $29,000,000 in 1873.   In Alabama, by 1874, the debt had mounted from $7,000,000 to $32,000,000.   The public debt of Louisiana rose from $14,000,000 in 1868 to $48,-000,000 in 1871, with a local debt of $31,000,000. Cities, towns, and counties sold bonds by the bale. The debt of New Orleans increased twenty-five fold and that of Vicksburg a thousandfold.   A great deal of the debt was the result of fraudulent issues of bonds or overissues. For this form of fraud the state financial agents in New York were usually

[1] Charles Nordhoff, *The Cotton States in the Spring and Summer of 1875.*

responsible. Southern bonds sold far below par, and the time came when they were peddled about at ten to twenty-five cents on the dollar.

Still another disastrous result followed this corrupt financiering. In Alabama there was a sixty-five per cent decrease in property values, in Florida forty-five per cent, and in Louisiana fifty to seventy-five per cent. A large part of the best property was mortgaged, and foreclosure sales were frequent. Poorer property could be neither mortgaged nor sold. There was an exodus of whites from the worst governed districts in the West and the North. Many towns, among them Mobile and Memphis, surrendered their charters and were ruled directly by the governor; and there were numerous "strangulated" counties which on account of debt had lost self-government and were ruled by appointees of the governor.

A part of the money raised by taxes and by bond sales was used for legitimate expenses and the rest went to pay forged warrants, excess warrants, and swollen mileage accounts, and to fill the pockets of embezzlers and thieves from one end of the South to the other. In Arkansas, for example, the auditor's clerk hire, which was $4000 in 1866, cost twenty-three times as much in 1873. In Louisiana and South Carolina stealing was elevated into an art and was practiced without concealment. In the latter State the worthless Hell Hole Swamp was bought for $26,000 to be farmed by the negroes but was charged to the State at $120,000. A free restaurant maintained at the Capitol for the legislators cost $125,000 for one session. The porter who conducted it said that he kept it open sixteen to twenty hours a day and that some one was always in the room eating and drinking or smoking. When a member left he would fill his pockets with cigars or with bottles of drink. Forty different brands of beverages were paid for by the State for the private use of members, and all sorts of food, furniture, and clothing were sent to the houses of members and were paid for by the State as "legislative supplies." On the bills appeared such items as imported mushrooms, one side of bacon, one feather bed, bustles, two pairs of extra long stockings, one pair of garters, one bottle perfume, twelve monogram cut glasses, one horse, one comb and brush, three gallons of whisky, one pair of corsets. During the recess, supplies were sent out to the rural homes of the members.

The endorsement of railroad securities by the State also furnished a source of easy money to

nest official and the crooked speculator.
Civil War, in response to the general de-
South for better railroad facilities, the
governments began to underwrite rail-
bonds.   When the carpetbag and negro governments came in, the policy was continued but
without proper safeguards.   Bonds were sometimes endorsed before the roads were constructed,
and even excess issues were authorized.   Bonds
were endorsed for some roads of which not a mile
was ever built.   The White River Valley and
Texas Railroad never came into existence, but it
obtained a grant of $175,000 from the State of
Arkansas.   Speaker Carter of the Louisiana Legislature received a financial interest in all railroad
endorsement bills which he steered through the
House.   Negro members were regularly bribed to
vote for the bond steals.   A witness swore that in
Louisiana it cost him $80,000 to get a railroad
charter passed, but that the Governor's signature
cost more than the consent of the Legislature.

When the roads defaulted on the payment of
interest, as most of them did, the burden fell upon
the State.   Not all of the blame for this perverted
legislation should be placed upon the corrupt
legislators, however, for the lawyers who saw the

bills through were frequently Southern Democrats representing supposedly respectable Northern capitalists. The railroads as well as the taxpayers suffered from this pernicious lobbying, for the companies were loaded with debts and rarely profited by the loans. Valuation of railroad property rapidly decreased. The roads of Alabama which were valued in 1871 at $26,000,000 had decreased in 1875 to $9,500,000.

The foundation of radical power in the South lay in the alienation of the races which had been accomplished between 1865 and 1868. To maintain this unhappy distrust, the radical leaders found an effective means in the negro militia. Under the constitution of every reconstructed State a negro constabulary was possible, but only in South Carolina, North Carolina, Louisiana, and Mississippi were the authorities willing to risk the dangers of arming the blacks. No governor dared permit the Southern whites to organize as militia. In South Carolina the carpetbag governor, Robert K. Scott, enrolled ninety-six thousand negroes as members of the militia and organized and armed twenty thousand of them. The few white companies were ordered to disband. In Louisiana the governor had a standing army of blacks called the Metropolitan Guard. In several States the negro militia was used as a constabulary and was sent to any part of the State to make arrests.

In spite of this provocation there were, after the riots of 1866–67, comparatively few race conflicts until reconstruction was drawing to a close. The intervening period was filled with the more peaceful activities of the Ku Klux Klan and the White Camelia.[1] But as the whites made up their minds to get rid of negro rule, the clashes came frequently and always ended in the death of more negroes than whites.[2] They would probably have continued with serious consequences if the whites had not eventually secured control of the government.

The lax election laws, framed indeed for the benefit of the party in power, gave the radicals ample opportunity to control the negro vote. The elections were frequently corrupt, though not a great deal of money was spent in bribery. It was found less expensive to use other methods of getting out the vote. The negroes were generally

[1] See pages 243–64.
[2] Among the bloodiest conflicts were those in Louisiana at Colfax, Coushatta, and New Orleans in 1873–74, and at Vicksburg and Clinton, Mississippi, in 1874–75.

made to understand that the Democrats wanted to put them back into slavery, but sometimes the leaders deemed it wiser to state more concretely that "Jeff Davis had come to Montgomery and is ready to organize the Confederacy again" if the Democrats should win; or to say that "if Carter is elected, he will not allow your wives and daughters to wear hoopskirts." In Alabama many thousand pounds of bacon and hams were sent in to be distributed among "flood sufferers" in a region which had not been flooded since the days of Noah. The negroes were told that they must vote right and receive enough bacon for a year, or "lose their rights" if they voted wrongly. Ballot-box stuffing developed into an art, and each negro was carefully inspected to see that he had the right kind of ticket before he was marched to the polls.

The inspection and counting of election returns were in the hands of the county and state boards, which were controlled by the governor, and which had authority to throw out or count in any number of votes. On the assumption that the radicals were entitled to all negro votes, the returning boards followed the census figures for the black population in order to arrive at the minimum radical vote. The action of the returning boards was specially flagrant in Louisiana and Florida and in the black counties of South Carolina.

Notwithstanding the fact that the very best arrangements had been made at Washington and in the States for the running of the radical machine, everywhere there were factional fights from the beginning. Usually the scalawags declared hostilities after they found that the carpetbaggers had control of the negroes and the inside track on the way to the best state and federal offices. Later, after the scalawags had for the most part left the radicals, there were contests among the carpetbaggers themselves for the control of the negro vote and the distribution of spoils. The defeated faction usually joined the Democrats. In Arkansas a split started in 1869 which by 1872 resulted in two state governments. Alabama in 1872 and Louisiana in 1874–75 each had two rival governments. This factionalism contributed largely to the overthrow of the radicals.

The radical structure, however, was still powerfully supported from without. Relations between the Federal Government and the state governments in the South were close, and the policy at Washington was frequently determined by conditions in the South. President Grant, though at first considerate, was usually consistently radical in his Southern policy.   This attitude is difficult to explain except by saying that Grant fell under the control of radical advisers after his break with Johnson, that his military instincts were offended by opposition in the South which his advisers told him was rebellious, and that he was impressed by the need of holding the Southern radical vote against the inroads of the Democrats. After about 1869 Grant never really understood the conditions in the South. He was content to control by means of Federal troops and thousands of deputy marshals. For this policy the Ku Klux activities gave sufficient excuse for a time, and the continued story of "rebel outrages" was always available to justify a call for soldiers or deputies. The enforcement legislation gave the color of law to any interference which was deemed necessary.

Federal troops served other ends than the mere preservation of order and the support of the radical state governments. They were used on occasion to decide between opposing factions and to oust conservatives who had forced their way into office. The army officers purged the Legislature of Georgia in 1870, that of Alabama in 1872, and that of Louisiana in 1875. In 1875 the city government of Vicksburg and the state government of Louisiana were overturned by the whites, but General Sheridan at once intervened to put back the negroes and carpetbaggers. He suggested to President Grant that the conservatives be declared "banditti" and he would make himself responsible for the rest. As soon as a State showed signs of going over to the Democrats or an important election was lost by the radicals, one House or the other of Congress in many instances sent an investigation committee to ascertain the reasons. The Committees on the Condition of the South or on the Late Insurrectionary States were nearly always ready with reports to establish the necessity of intervention.

Besides the army there was in every State a powerful group of Federal officials who formed a "ring" for the direction of all good radicals. These marshals, deputies, postmasters, district attorneys, and customhouse officials were in close touch with Washington and frequently dictated nominations and platforms. At New Orleans the officials acted as a committee on credentials and held all the state conventions under their control in the customhouse.

Such was the machinery used to sustain a party

which, with the gradual defection of the whites, became throughout the South almost uniformly black. At first few negroes asked for offices, but soon the carpetbaggers found it necessary to divide with the rapidly growing number of negro politicians. No negro was elected governor, though several reached the office of lieutenant governor, secretary of state, auditor, superintendent of education, justice of the state supreme court, and fifteen were elected to Congress.[1] It would not be correct to say that the negro race was malicious or on evil bent. Unless deliberately stirred up by white leaders, few negroes showed signs of mean spirit. Few even made exorbitant demands. They wanted "something" — schools and freedom and "something else," they knew not what. Deprived of the leadership of the best whites, they could not possibly act with the scalawags — their traditional enemies. Nothing was left for them but to follow the carpetbagger.

[1] Revels, Lynch, and Bruce represent the better negro officeholders; Pinchback, Rainey, and Nash, the less respectable ones; and below these were the rascals whose ambition was to equal their white preceptors in corruption.

CHAPTER XI

THE Ku Klux movement, which took the form of secret revolutionary societies, grew out of a general conviction among the whites that the reconstruction policies were impossible and not to be endured. Somers, an English traveler, says that at this time "nearly every respectable white man in the Southern States was not only disfranchised but under fear of arrest or confiscation; the old foundations of authority were utterly razed before any new ones had yet been laid, and in the dark and benighted interval the remains of the Confederate armies — swept after a long and heroic day of fair fight from the field — flitted before the eyes of the people in this weird and midnight shape of a Ku Klux Klan." Ryland Randolph, an Alabama editor who was also an official of the Klan, stated in his paper that "the origin of Ku Klux Klan is in the galling despotism that broods like a night-mare over these Southern States — a fungus growth of military tyranny superinduced by the fostering of Loyal Leagues, the abrogation of our civil laws, the habitual violation of our national Constitution, and a persistent prostitution of all government, all resources and all powers, to degrade the white man by the establishment of negro supremacy."

The secret orders, regardless of their original purposes, were all finally to be found opposing radical reconstruction. Everywhere their objects were the same: to recover for the white race their former control of society and government, and to destroy the baneful influence of the alien among the blacks. The people of the South were by law helpless to take steps towards setting up any kind of government in a land infested by a vicious element — Federal and Confederate deserters, bushwhackers, outlaws of every description, and negroes, some of whom proved insolent and violent in their newly found freedom. Nowhere was property or person safe, and for a time many feared a negro insurrection. General Hardee said to his neighbors, "I advise you to get ready for what may come. We are standing over a sleeping volcano."

To cope with this situation ante-bellum patrols

— the "patter-rollers" as the negroes called them — were often secretly reorganized. In each community for several months after the Civil War, and in many of them for months before the end of the war, there were informal vigilance committees. Some of these had such names as the Black Cavalry and Men of Justice in Alabama, the Home Guards in many other places, while the anti-Confederate societies of the war, the Heroes of America, the Red Strings, and the Peace Societies, transformed themselves in certain localities into regulatory bodies. Later these secret societies numbered scores, perhaps hundreds, varying from small bodies of local police to great federated bodies which covered almost the entire South and even had membership in the North and West. Other important organizations were the Constitutional Union Guards, the Pale Faces, the White Brotherhood, the Council of Safety, the '76 Association, the Sons of '76, the Order of the White Rose, and the White Boys. As the fight against reconstruction became bolder, the orders threw off their disguises and appeared openly as armed whites fighting for the control of society. The White League of Louisiana, the White Line of Mississippi, the White Man's party of Alabama, and the Rifle

Clubs of South Carolina, were later manifestations of the general Ku Klux movement.

The two largest secret orders, however, were the Ku Klux Klan, from which the movement took its name, and the Knights of the White Camelia. The Ku Klux Klan originated at Pulaski, Tennessee, in the autumn of 1865, as a local organization for social purposes. The founders were young Confederates, united for fun and mischief. The name was an accidental corruption of the Greek word *Kuklos*, a circle. The officers adopted queer sounding titles and strange disguises. Weird night riders in ghostly attire thoroughly frightened the superstitious negroes, who were told that the spirits of dead Confederates were abroad. This terrorizing of the blacks successfully provided the amusement which the founders desired and there were many applications for admission to the society. The Pulaski Club, or Den, was in the habit of parading in full uniform at social gatherings of the whites at night, much to the delight of the small boys and girls. Pulaski was near the Alabama line, and many of the young men of Alabama who saw these parades or heard of them organized similar Dens in the towns of Northern Alabama. Nothing but horseplay, however, took place at the meetings. In 1867 and 1868 the order appeared in parade in the towns of the adjoining States and, as we are told, "cut up curious gyrations" on the public squares.

There was a general belief outside the order that there was a purpose behind all the ceremonial and frolic of the Dens; many joined the order convinced that its object was serious; others saw the possibilities of using it as a means of terrorizing the negroes. After men discovered the power of the Klan over the negroes, indeed, they were generally inclined, owing to the disordered conditions of the time, to act as a sort of police patrol and to hold in check the thieving negroes, the Union League, and the "loyalists." In this way, from being merely a number of social clubs the Dens swiftly became bands of regulators, taking on many new fantastic qualities along with their new seriousness of purpose. Some of the more ardent spirits led the Dens far in the direction of violence and outrage. Attempts were made by the parent Den at Pulaski to regulate the conduct of the others, but, owing to the loose organization, the effort met with little success. Some of the Dens, indeed, lost all connection with the original order.

A general organization of these societies was

perfected at a convention held in Nashville in May, 1867, just as the Reconstruction Acts were being put into operation.   A constitution called the *Prescript* was adopted which provided for a national organization.   The former slave States, except Delaware, constituted the Empire, which was ruled by the Grand Wizard (then General Forrest) with a staff of ten Genii; each State was a realm under a Grand Dragon and eight Hydras; the next subdivision was a Dominion, consisting of several counties, ruled by a Grand Titan and six Furies; the county or Province was governed by a Grand Giant and four Goblins; the unit was the Den or community organization, of which there might be several in each county, each under a Grand Cyclops and two Nighthawks.   The Genii, Hydras, Furies, Goblins, and Nighthawks were staff officers.   The private members were called Ghouls.   The order had no name, and at first was designated by two stars (**), later by three (***).   Sometimes it was called the Invisible Empire of Ku Klux Klan.

Any white man over eighteen might be admitted to the Den after nomination by a member and strict investigation by a committee.   The oath demanded obedience and secrecy.   The Dens governed themselves by the ordinary rules of deliberative bodies.   The punishment for betrayal of secrecy was "the extreme penalty of the Law." None of the secrets was to be written, and there was a "Register" of alarming adjectives, such as terrible, horrible, furious, doleful, bloody, appalling, frightful, gloomy, which was used as a cipher code in dating the odd Ku Klux orders.

The general objects of the order were thus set forth in the revised *Prescript:* first, to protect the weak, the innocent, and the defenseless from the indignities, wrongs, and outrages of the lawless, the violent, and the brutal; to relieve the injured and oppressed; to succor the suffering and unfortunate, and especially the widows and orphans of Confederate soldiers; second, to protect and defend the Constitution of the United States and all laws passed in conformity thereto, and to protect the States and people thereof from all invasion from any source whatever; third, to aid and assist in the execution of all "constitutional" laws, and to protect the people from unlawful arrest, and from trial except by their peers according to the laws of the land.   But the tests for admission gave further indication of the objects of the order.   No Republican, no Union Leaguer, and no member of the G. A. R. might become a member.   The members were pledged to oppose negro equality of any kind, to favor emancipation of the Southern whites and the restoration of their rights, and to maintain constitutional government and equitable laws.

Prominent men testified that the order became popular because the whites felt that they were persecuted and that there was no legal protection, no respectable government. General (later Senator) Pettus said that through all the workings of the Federal Government ran the principle that "we are an inferior, degraded people and not fit to be trusted." General Clanton of Alabama further explained that "there is not a respectable white woman in the Negro Belt of Alabama who will trust herself outside of her house without some protector. . . . So far as our State Government is concerned, we are in the hands of camp-followers, horse-holders, cooks, bottle-washers, and thieves. . . . We have passed out from the hands of the brave soldiers who overcame us, and are turned over to the tender mercies of squaws for torture. . . . I see negro police — great black fellows — leading white girls around the streets of Montgomery, and locking them up in jails."

The Klan first came into general prominence in 1868 with the report of the Federal commanders in the South concerning its activities.   Soon after that date the order spread through the white counties of the South, in many places absorbing the White Brotherhood, the Pale Faces, and some other local organizations which had been formed in the upper part of the Black Belt.   But it was not alone in the field.   The order known as the Knights of the White Camelia, founded in Louisiana in 1867 and formally organized in 1868, spread rapidly over the lower South until it reached the territory occupied by the Ku Klux Klan.   It was mainly a Black Belt order, and on the whole had a more substantial and more conservative membership than the other large secret bodies.   Like the Ku Klux Klan, it also absorbed several minor local societies.

The White Camelia had a national organization with headquarters in New Orleans.   Its business was conducted by a Supreme Council of the United States, with Grand, Central, and Subordinate Councils for each State, county, and community. All communication within the order took place by passwords and cipher; the organization and the officers were similar to those of the Ku Klux Klan; and all officers were designated by initials.   An ex-member states that "during the three years of its existence here [Perry County, Alabama] I believe its organization and discipline were as perfect as human ingenuity could have made it." The fundamental object of the White Camelia was the "maintenance of the supremacy of the white race," and to this end the members were constrained "to observe a marked distinction between the races" and to restrain the "African race to that condition of social and political inferiority for which God has destined it." The members were pledged to vote only for whites, to oppose negro equality in all things, but to respect the legitimate rights of negroes.

The smaller orders were similar in purpose and organization to the Ku Klux Klan and the White Camelia. Most of them joined or were affiliated with the large societies. Probably a majority of the men of the South were associated at some time during this period with these revolutionary bodies. As a rule the politicians, though approving, held aloof. Public opinion generally supported the movement so long as the radicals made serious attempts to carry out the reconstruction policies.

The task before the secret orders was to regulate the conduct of the blacks and their leaders in order that honor, life, and property might be secure. They planned to accomplish this aim by playing upon the fears, superstitions, and cowardice of the black race — in a word, by creating a white terror to counteract the black one. To this end they made use of strange disguises, mysterious and fearful conversation, midnight rides and drills, and silent parades. As long as secrecy and mystery were to be effective in dealing with the negroes, costume was an important matter. These disguises varied with the locality and often with the individual. High cardboard hats, covered with white cloth often decorated with stars or pictures of animals, white masks with holes cut for eyes, nose and mouth bound with red braid to give a horrible appearance, and frequently a long tongue of red flannel so fixed that it could be moved with the wearer's tongue, and a long white robe — these made up a costume which served at the same time as a disguise and as a means of impressing the impressionable negro. Horses were covered with sheets or white cloth held on by the saddle and by belts, and sometimes the animals were even painted. Skulls of sheep and cattle, and even of human beings were often carried on the saddlebows to add another element of terror. A framework was sometimes made to fit the shoulders of a Ghoul which caused him to appear twelve feet high. A skeleton wooden hand at the end of a stick served to greet terrified negroes at midnight. For safety every man carried a small whistle and a brace of pistols.

The trembling negro who ran into a gathering of the Ku Klux on his return from a Loyal League meeting was informed that the white-robed figures he saw were the spirits of the Confederate dead killed at Chickamauga or Shiloh, now unable to rest in their graves because of the conduct of the negroes. He was told in a sepulchral voice of the necessity for his remaining more at home and taking a less active part in predatory excursions abroad. In the middle of the night a sleeping negro might wake to find his house surrounded by a ghostly company, or to see several terrifying figures standing by his bedside. They were, they said, the ghosts of men whom he had formerly known. They had scratched through from Hell to warn the negroes of the consequences of their misconduct. Hell was a dry and thirsty land; and they asked him for water. Bucket after bucket of water disappeared into a sack of leather, rawhide, or rubber, concealed within the flowing robe. The story is told of one of these night travelers who called at the cabin of a radical negro in Attakapas

County, Louisiana. After drinking three buckets of water to the great astonishment of the darky, the traveler thanked him and told him that he had traveled nearly a thousand miles within twenty-four hours, and that that was the best water he had tasted since he was killed at the battle of Shiloh. The negro dropped the bucket, overturned chairs and table in making his escape through the window, and was never again seen or heard of by residents of that community. Another incident is told of a parade in Pulaski, Tennessee: "While the procession was passing a corner on which a negro man was standing, a tall horseman in hideous garb turned aside from the line, dismounted and stretched out his bridle rein toward the negro, as if he desired him to hold his horse. Not daring to refuse, the frightened African extended his hand to grasp the rein. As he did so, the Ku Klux took his own head from his shoulders and offered to place that also in the outstretched hand. The negro stood not upon the order of his going, but departed with a yell of terror. To this day he will tell you: 'He done it, suah, boss. I seed him do it.'"

It was seldom necessary at this early stage to use violence, for the black population was in an ecstasy of fear. A silent host of white-sheeted horsemen parading the country roads at night was sufficient to reduce the blacks to good behavior for weeks or months.   One silent Ghoul posted near a meeting place of the League would be the cause of the immediate dissolution of that club.   Cow bones in a sack were rattled within earshot of the terrified negroes.   A horrible being, fifteen feet tall, walking through the night toward a place of congregation, was very likely to find that every one had vacated the place before he arrived.   A few figures wrapped in sheets and sitting on tombstones in a graveyard near which negroes were accustomed to pass would serve to keep the immediate community quiet for weeks and give the locality a reputation for "hants" which lasted long.

To prevent detection on parade, members of the Klan often stayed out of the parade in their own town and were to be seen freely and conspicuously mingling with the spectators.   A man who believed that he knew every horse in the vicinity and was sure that he would be able to identify the riders by their horses was greatly surprised upon lifting the disguise of the horse nearest him to find the animal upon which he himself had ridden into town a short while before.   The parades were always silent and so arranged as to give the impression of very large numbers.   In the regular drills which were held in town and country the men showed that they had not forgotten their training in the Confederate army.   There were no commands save in a very low tone or in a mysterious language, and usually only signs or whistle signals were used.

Such pacific methods were successful to a considerable degree until the carpetbaggers and scalawags were placed in office under the Reconstruction Acts.   Then more violent methods were necessary. The Klans patrolled disturbed communities, visited, warned, and frightened obnoxious individuals, whipped some, and even hanged others.   Until forbidden by law or military order, the newspapers were accustomed to print the mysterious proclamations of the Ku Klux.   The following, which was circulated in Montgomery, Alabama, in April, 1868, is a typical specimen:

K. K. K.
Clan of Vega.
HDQR'S K. K. K. HOSPITALLERS.
Vega Clan, New Moon,
3rd Month, Anno K. K. K. 1.

ORDER No. K. K.
Clansmen — Meet at the Trysting Spot when Orion Kisses the Zenith.   The doom of treason is Death. *Dies Iræ.*   The wolf is on his walk — the serpent coils

17

to strike. Action! Action!! Action!!! By midnight and the Tomb; by Sword and Torch and the Sacred Oath at Forrester's Altar, I bid you come! The
clansmen of Glen Iran and Alpine will greet you at the
new-made grave.

Remember the Ides of April.

By command of the Grand D. I. H.

Cheg. V.

The work of the secret orders was successful. As
bodies of vigilantes, the Klans and the Councils
regulated the conduct of bad negroes, punished
criminals who were not punished by the State,
looked after the activities and teachings of Northern preachers and teachers, dispersed hostile gatherings of negroes, and ran out of the community the
worst of the reconstructionist officials. They kept
the negroes quiet and freed them to some extent
from the influence of evil leaders. The burning
of houses, gins, mills, and stores ceased; property
became more secure; people slept safely at night;
women and children walked abroad in security; the
incendiary agents who had worked among the
negroes left the country; agitators, political, educational, and religious, became more moderate; "bad
niggers" ceased to be bad; labor became less disorganized; the carpetbaggers and scalawags ceased
to batten on the Southern communities. It was

not so much a revolution as the defeat of a revolution. Society was replaced in the old historic grooves from which war and reconstruction had jarred it.

Successful as was the Ku Klux movement in these respects, it had at the same time many harmful results. Too often local orders fell under the control of reckless or lawless men and the Klan was then used as a cloak to cover violence and thievery; family and personal feuds were carried into the orders and fought out; and anti-negro feeling in many places found expression in activities designed to drive the blacks from the country. It was easy for any outlaw to hide himself behind the protection of a secret order. So numerous did these men become that after 1868 there was a general exodus of the leading reputable members, and in 1869 the formal disbanding of the Klan was proclaimed by General Forrest, the Grand Wizard. The White Camelia and other orders also gradually went out of existence. Numerous attempts were made to suppress the secret movement by the military commanders, the state governments, and finally by Congress, but none of these was entirely successful, for in each community the secret opposition lasted as long as it was needed.

The political effects of the orders, however, survived their organized existence. Some of the
Southern States began to go Democratic in spite of
the Reconstruction Acts and the Amendments, and
there was little doubt that the Ku Klux movement
had aided in this change. In order to preserve the
achievements of radical reconstruction Congress
passed, in 1870 and 1871, the enforcement acts
which had been under debate for nearly two years.
The first act (May 31, 1870) was designed to protect the negro's right to vote and was directed at
individuals as well as against States. Section six,
indeed, was aimed specifically at the Ku Klux Klan.
This act was a long step in the direction of giving
the Federal Government control over state elections. But as North Carolina went wholly and
Alabama partially Democratic in 1870, a Supplementary Act (February 28, 1871) went further and
placed the elections for members of Congress completely under Federal control, and also authorized
the use of thousands of deputy marshals at elections. As the campaign of 1872 drew near, Grant
and his advisers became solicitous to hold all the
Southern States which had not been regained by
the Democrats. Accordingly, on March 23, 1871,
the President sent a message to Congress declaring

that in some of the States the laws could not be enforced and asked for remedial legislation. Congress responded with an act (April 20, 1871), commonly called the "Ku Klux Act," which gave the President despotic military power to uphold the remaining negro governments and authorized him to declare a state of war when he considered it necessary. Of this power Grant made use in only one instance. In October, 1871, he declared nine counties of South Carolina in rebellion and put them under martial law.

During the ten years following 1870, several thousand arrests were made under the enforcement acts and about 1250 convictions were secured, principally in Mississippi, North Carolina, South Carolina, and Tennessee. Most of these violations of election laws, however, had nothing to do with the Ku Klux movement, for by 1870 the better class of members had withdrawn from the secret orders. But though the enforcement acts checked these irregularities to a considerable extent, they nevertheless failed to hold the South for the radicals and essential parts of them were declared unconstitutional a few years later.

In order to justify the passage of the enforcement acts and to obtain campaign material for use in 1872, Congress appointed a committee, organized on the very day when the Ku Klux Act was approved, to investigate conditions in the Southern States. From June to August, 1871, the committee took testimony in Washington, and in the fall subcommittees visited several Southern States. Tennessee, Virginia, Arkansas, Louisiana, and Texas were, however, omitted from the investigation. Notwithstanding the partisan purpose and methods of the investigation, the report of the committee and the accompanying testimony constituted a Democratic rather than a Republican document. It is a veritable mine of information about the South between 1865 and 1871. The Democratic minority members made skillful use of their opportunity to expose conditions in the South. They were less concerned to meet the charges made against the Ku Klux Klan than to show why such movements came about. The Republicans, concerned mainly about material for the presidential campaign, neglected the broader phases of the situation.

Opposition to the effects of reconstruction did not come to an end with the dissolution of the more famous orders. On the contrary, it now became public and open and resulted in the organization, after 1872, of the White League, the Mississippi Shot Gun Plan, the White Man's Party in Alabama, and the Rifle Clubs in South Carolina. The later movements were distinctly but cautiously anti-negro. There was most irritation in the white counties where there were large numbers of negroes. Negro schools and churches were burned because they served as meeting places for negro political organizations. The color line began to be more and more sharply drawn. Social and business ostracism continued to be employed against white radicals, while the negroes were discharged from employment or were driven from their rented farms.

The Ku Klux movement, it is to be noted in retrospect, originated as an effort to restore order in the war-stricken Southern States. The secrecy of its methods appealed to the imagination and caused its rapid expansion, and this secrecy was inevitable because opposition to reconstruction was not lawful. As the reconstruction policies were put into operation, the movement became political and used violence when appeals to superstitious fears ceased to be effective. The Ku Klux Klan centered, directed, and crystallized public opinion, and united the whites upon a platform of white

supremacy. The Southern politicians stood aloof
from the movement but accepted the results of its
work. It frightened the negroes and bad whites into
better conduct, and it encouraged the conservatives
and aided them to regain control of society, for without the operations of the Klan the black districts
would never have come again under white control.
Towards the end, however, its methods frequently
became unnecessarily violent and did great harm to
Southern society. The Ku Klux system of regulating society is as old as history; it had often been
used before; it may even be used again. When a
people find themselves persecuted by aliens under
legal forms, they will invent some means outside
the law for protecting themselves; and such experiences will inevitably result in a weakening of respect
for law and in a return to more primitive methods
of justice.

CHAPTER XII

THE CHANGING SOUTH

"THE bottom rail is on top" was a phrase which had flashed throughout the late Confederate States. It had been coined by the negroes in 1867 to express their view of the situation, but its aptness had been recognized by all. After ten years of social and economic revolution, however, it was not so clear that the phrase of 1867 correctly described the new situation. "The white man made free" would have been a more accurate epitome, for the white man had been able, in spite of his temporary disabilities, to compete with the negro in all industries.

It will be remembered that the negro districts were least exposed to the destruction of war. The well-managed plantation, lying near the highways of commerce, with its division of labor, nearly or quite self-sufficing, was the bulwark of the Confederacy. When the fighting ended, an industrial revolution began in these untouched parts of the

Black Belt.   The problem of free negro labor now
appeared.   During the year 1865 no general plan
for a labor system was formulated except by the
Freedmen's Bureau.   That, however, was not a
success.   There were all sorts of makeshifts, such as
cash wages, deferred wages, coöperation, even shar-
ing of expense and product, and contracts, either
oral or written.

The employers showed a disposition to treat the
negro family as a unit in making contracts for labor, wages, food, clothes, and care.[1]   In general
these early arrangements were made to transform
slavery with its mutual duties and obligations into
a free labor system with wages and "privileges."
The "privileges" of slavery could not be destroyed;
in fact, they have never yet been destroyed in numerous places.   Curious demands were made by the
negroes: here, farm bells must not ring; there, overseers or managers must be done away with; in
some places plantation courts were to settle matters of work, rent, and conduct; elsewhere, agreements were made that on Saturday the laborer

[1] J. D. B. De Bow, the economist, testified before the Joint Committee on Reconstruction that, if the negro would work, free labor
would be better for the planters than slave labor.   He called attention to the fact, however, that negro women showed a desire to avoid
field labor, and there is also evidence to show that they objected to
domestic service and other menial work.

should be permitted to go to town and, perhaps, ride a mule or horse. In South Carolina the Sea Island negroes demanded that in laying out work the old "tasks" or "stints" of slavery days be retained as the standard. The farming districts at the edge of the Black Belt, where the races were about equal in numbers, already had a kind of "share system," and in these sections the economic chaos after the war was not so complete. The former owners worked in the field with their ex-slaves and thus provided steady employment for many. Farms were rented for a fixed sum of money, or for a part of the crop, or on "shares."

The white districts, which had previously fought a losing competition with the efficiently managed and inexpensive slave labor of the Black Belt, were affected most disastrously by war and its after-math. They were distant from transportation lines and markets; they employed poor farming methods; they had no fertilizers; they raised no staple crops on their infertile land; and in addi-tion they now had to face the destitution that follows fighting. Yet these regions had formerly been almost self-supporting, although the farms were small and no elaborate labor system had been developed.

In the planting districts where the owner was land-poor he made an attempt to bring in Northern capital and Northern or foreign labor. In the belief that the negroes would work better for a Northern man, every planter who could do so secured a Northern partner or manager, frequently a soldier. Nevertheless these imported managers nearly always failed because they did not understand cotton, rice, or sugar planting, and because they were either too severe or too easy upon the blacks.

No Northern labor was to be had, and the South could not retain even all its own native whites. Union soldiers and others seeking to better their prospects moved west and northwest to fill the newly opened lands, while the Confederates, kept out of the homestead region by the test oath, swarmed into Texas, which owned its own public lands, or went North to other occupations. Nor could the desperate planters hire foreign immigrants. Several States, among them South Carolina, Alabama, and Louisiana, advertised for laborers and established labor bureaus, but without avail. The negro politicians in 1867 declared themselves opposed to all movements to foster immigration. So in the Black Belt the negro had, for forty years, a monopoly of farm labor.

The share system of tenantry, with its attendant evils of credit and crop lien, was soon established in the Southern States, mainly in the Black Belt, but to some extent also in the white districts. The landlord furnished land, house, fuel, water, and all or a part of the seed, fertilizer, farm implements, and farm animals. In return he received a "half," or a "third and fourth," his share depending upon how much he had furnished. The best class of tenants would rent for cash or a fixed rental, the poorest laborers would work for wages only.

The "privileges" brought over from slavery, which were included in the share renting, astonished outside observers. To the laborer was usually given a house, a water supply, wood for fuel, pasture for pigs or cows, a "patch" for vegetables and fruit, and the right to hunt and fish. These were all that some needed in order to live. Somers, the English traveler already quoted, pronounced this generous custom "outrageously absurd," for the negroes had so many privileges that they refused to make use of their opportunities. "The soul is often crushed out of labor by penury and oppression," he said, "but here a soul cannot begin to be infused into it through the sheer excess of privilege and license with which it is surrounded."

The credit system which was developed beside the share system made a bad condition worse. On the 1st of January a planter could mortgage his future crop to a merchant or landlord in exchange for subsistence until the harvest. Since, as a rule, neither tenant nor landlord had any surplus funds, the latter would be supplied by the banker or banker merchant, who would then dictate the crops to be planted and the time of sale. As a result of these conditions, the planter or farmer was held to staple crops, high prices for necessities, high interest rate, and frequently unfair bookkeeping. The system was excellent for a thrifty, industrious, and intelligent man, for it enabled him to get a start. It worked to the advantage of a bankrupt landlord, who could in this way get banking facilities. But it had a mischievous effect upon the average tenant, who had too small a share of the crop to feel a strong sense of responsibility as well as too many "privileges" and too little supervision to make him anxious to produce the best results.

The negroes entered into their freedom with several advantages: they were trained to labor; they were occupying the most fertile soil and could purchase land at low prices; the tenant system was most liberal; cotton, sugar, and rice were bringing high prices; and access to markets was easy. In the white districts land was cheap, and prices of commodities were high, but otherwise the negroes seemed to have the better position. Yet as early as 1870, keen observers called attention to the fact that the hill and mountain whites were thriving as compared with their former condition, and that the negroes were no longer their serious competitors. In the white districts better methods were coming into use, labor was steady, fertilizers were used, and conditions of transportation were improving. The whites were also encroaching on the Black Belt; they were opening new lands in the Southwest; and within the border of the Black Belt they were bringing negro labor under some control. In the South Carolina rice lands, crowds of Irish were imported to do the ditching which the negroes refused to do and were carried back North when the job was finished.[1] President Thach

[1] The Census of 1880 gave proof of the superiority of the whites in cotton production. For purposes of comparison the cotton area may be divided into three regions: first, the Black Belt, in which the farmers were black, the soil fertile, the plantations large, the credit evil at its worst, and the yield of cotton per acre the least; second, the white districts, where the soil was the poorest, the farms small, the workers nearly all white, and the yield per acre better than on the fertile Black Belt lands; third, the regions in which the races were nearly equal in

of the Alabama Agricultural College has thus described the situation:

By the use of commercial fertilizers, vast regions once considered barren have been brought into profitable cultivation, and really afford a more reliable and constant crop than the rich alluvial lands of the old slave plantations.   In nearly every agricultural county in the South there is to be observed, on the one hand, this section of fertile soils, once the heart of the old civilization, now abandoned by the whites, held in tenantry by a dense negro population, full of dilapidation and ruin; while on the other hand, there is the region of light, thin soils, occupied by the small white freeholder, filled with schools, churches, and good roads, and all the elements of a happy, enlightened country life.

All the systems devised for handling negro labor proved to be only partially successful.   The laborer was migratory, wanted easy work, with one or two holidays a week, and the privilege of attending political meetings, camp meetings, and circuses.   A thrifty negro could not make headway because his fellows stole from him or his less energetic relations and friends visited him and ate up

numbers or where the whites were in a slight majority, with soil of medium fertility, good methods of agriculture, and, owing to better controlled labor, the best yield.   In other words, negroes, fertile soil, and poor crops went together; and on the other hand the whites got better crops on less fertile soil.   The Black Belt has never again reached the level of production it had in 1860.   But the white district kept improving slowly.

his substance. One Alabama planter declared that he could not raise a turkey, a chicken, a hog, or a cow; and another asserted that "a hog has no more chance to live among these thieving negro farmers than a June bug in a gang of puddle ducks." Lands were mortgaged to the supply houses in the towns, the whites gradually deserted the country, and many rice and cotton fields grew up in weeds. Crop stealing at night became a business which no legislation could ever completely stop.

A traveler has left the following description of "a model negro farm" in 1874. The farmer purchased an old mule on credit and rented land on shares or for so many bales of cotton; any old tools were used; corn, bacon, and other supplies were bought on credit, and a crop lien was given; a month later, corn and cotton were planted on soil that was not well broken up; the negro "would not pay for no guano" to put on other people's land; by turns the farmer planted and fished, plowed and hunted, hoed and frolicked, or went to "meeting." At the end of the year he sold his cotton, paid part of his rent and some of his debt, returned the mule to its owner, and sang:

> Nigger work hard all de year,
> White man tote de money.

The great landholdings did not break up into small farms as was predicted, though sales were frequent and in 1865 enormous amounts of land were put on the market. After 1867, additional millions of acres were offered at small prices, and tax and mortgage sales were numerous. The result of these operations, however, was a change of landlords rather than a breaking up of large plantations. New men, negroes, merchants, and Jews became landowners. The number of small farms naturally increased but so in some instances did the land concentrated into large holdings.

It was inevitable that conditions of negro life should undergo a revolutionary change during the reconstruction. The serious matter of looking out for himself and his family and of making a living dampened the negro's cheerful spirits. Released from the discipline of slavery and often misdirected by the worst of teachers, the negro race naturally ran into excesses of petty criminality. Even under the reconstruction governments the proportion of negro to white criminals was about ten to one. Theft was frequent; arson was the accepted means of revenge on white people; and murder became common in the brawls of the city negro quarters. The laxness of the marriage relation worked special hardship on the women and children in so many cases deserted by the head of the family.

Out of the social anarchy of reconstruction the negroes emerged with numerous organizations of their own which may have been imitations of the Union League, the Lincoln Brotherhood, and the various church organizations. These societies were composed entirely of blacks and have continued with prolific reproduction to the present day. They were characterized by high names, gorgeous regalia, and frequent parades. "The Brothers and Sisters of Pleasure and Prosperity" and the "United Order of African Ladies and Gentlemen" played a large, and on the whole useful, part in negro social life, teaching lessons of thrift, insurance, coöperation, and mutual aid.

The reconstructionists were not able in 1867–68 to carry through Congress any provision for the social equality of the races, but in the reconstructed States the equal rights issue was alive throughout the period. Legislation giving to the negro equal rights in hotels, places of amusements, and common carriers, was first enacted in Louisiana and South Carolina. Frequently the carpetbaggers brought up the issue in order to rid the radical ranks of the scalawags who were opposed to equal rights. In Florida, for example, the carpetbaggers framed a comprehensive Equal Rights Law, passed it, and presented it to Governor Reed, who was known to be opposed to such legislation. He vetoed the measure and thus lost the negro support. Intermarriage with whites was made legal in Louisiana and South Carolina and by court decision was permitted in Alabama and Mississippi, but the Georgia Supreme Court held it to be illegal. Mixed marriages were few, but these were made occasions of exultation over the whites and of consequent ill feeling.

Charles Sumner was a persistent agitator for equal rights. In 1871 he declared in a letter to a South Carolina negro convention that the race must insist not only upon equality in hotels and on public carriers but also in the schools. "It is not enough," he said, "to provide separate accommodations for colored citizens even if in all respects as good as those of other persons. . . . The discrimination is an insult and a hindrance, and a bar, which not only destroys comfort and prevents equality, but weakens all other rights. The right to vote will have new security when your equal right in public conveyances, hotels, and common schools, is at last established; but here you must insist for yourselves by speech, petition, and by vote." The Southern whites began to develop the "Jim Crow" theory of "separate but equal" accommodations. Senator Hill of Georgia, for example, thought that hotels might have separate divisions for the two races, and he cited the division in the churches as proof that the negro wanted separation.

About 1874 it was plain that the last radical Congress was nearly ready to enact social equality legislation. This fact turned many of the Southern Unionist class back to the Democratic party, there to remain for a long time. In 1875, as a sort of memorial to Sumner, Congress passed the Civil Rights Act, which gave to negroes equal rights in hotels, places of amusement, on public carriers, and on juries. Some Democratic leaders were willing to see such legislation enacted, because in the first place, it would have little effect except in the Border and Northern States, where it would turn thousands into the Democratic fold, and in the second place, because they were sure that in time the Supreme Court would declare the law unconstitutional. And so it happened.

In regions where the more unprincipled radical leaders were in control, the whites lived at times in fear of negro uprisings. The negroes were armed

and insolent, and the whites were few and widely
scattered.   Here and there outbreaks occurred and
individual whites and isolated families suffered,
but as a rule all such movements were crushed with
much heavier loss to the negroes than to the better
organized whites.   Nevertheless everlasting appre-
hension for the safety of women and children kept
the white men nervous.   General Garnett Andrews
remarked about the situation in Mississippi:

I have never suffered such an amount of anguish and
alarm in all my life.   I have served through the whole
war as a soldier in the army of Northern Virginia, and
saw all of it; but I never did experience . . . the fear
and alarm and sense of danger which I felt that time.
And this was the universal feeling among the population,
among the white people.   I think that both sides were
alarmed and felt uneasy.   It showed itself upon the
countenance of the people; it made many of them sick.
Men looked haggard and pale, after undergoing this
sort of thing for six weeks or a month, and I have felt
when I laid [sic] down that neither myself, nor my wife
and children were in safety.   I expected, and honestly
anticipated, and thought it highly probable, that I
might be assassinated and my house set on fire at
any time.

By the fires of reconstruction the whites were
fused into a more homogeneous society, social as
well as political.   The former slaveholding class

continued to be more considerate of the negro than were the poor whites; but, as misrule went on, all classes tended to unite against the negro in politics. They were tired of reconstruction, new amendments, force bills, Federal troops — tired of being ruled as conquered provinces by the incompetent and the dishonest. Every measure aimed at the South seemed to them to mean that they were considered incorrigible and unworthy of trust, and that they were being made to suffer for the deeds of irresponsible whites. And, to make matters worse, strong opposition to proscriptive measures was called fresh rebellion. "When the Jacobins say and do low and bitter things, their charge of want of loyalty in the South because our people grumble back a little seems to me as unreasonable as the complaint of the little boy: 'Mamma, make Bob 'have hisself. He makes mouths at me every time I hit him with my stick.'"[1]

Probably this burden fell heavier on the young men, who had life before them and who were growing up with diminished opportunities. Sidney Lanier, then an Alabama school-teacher, wrote to Bayard Taylor: "Perhaps you know that with us

[1] Usually ascribed to General D. H. Hill of North Carolina, and quoted in *The Land We Love*, vol. I, p. 146.

of the young generation in the South, since the war, pretty much the whole of life has been merely not dying." Negro and alien rule was a constant insult to the intelligence of the country. The taxpayers were nonparticipants in the affairs of government. Some people withdrew entirely from public life, went to their farms or plantations, kept away from towns and from speechmaking, waiting for the end to come. There were some who refused for several years to read the newspapers, so unpleasant was the news. The good feeling produced by the magnanimity of Grant at Appomattox was destroyed by the severity of his Southern policy when he became President. There was no gratitude for any so-called leniency of the North, no repentance for the war, no desire for humiliation, for sackcloth and ashes, and no confession of wrong. The insistence of the radicals upon obtaining a confession of depravity only made things much worse. Scarcely a measure of Congress during reconstruction was designed or received in a conciliatory spirit.

The new generation of whites was poor, bitter because of persecution, ill educated, overworked, without a bright future, and shadowed by the race problem. Though their new political leaders were

shrewd, narrow, conservative, honest, and parsi-
monious, the constant fighting of fire with fire
scorched all.   In the bitter discipline of reconstruction, the pleasantest side of Southern life came to
an end.   During the war and the consequent reconstruction there was a marked change in Southern temperament toward the severe.   Hospitality
declined; the old Southern life had never been
on a business basis, but the new Southern life now
adjusted itself to a stricter economy; the old in-
dividuality was partially lost; but class distinc-
tions were less obvious in a more homogeneous
society.   The material evils of reconstruction may
be only temporary; state debts may be paid and
wasted resources renewed; but the moral and
intellectual results of the revolution will be the
more permanent.

CHAPTER XIII

RESTORATION OF HOME RULE

THE radical program of reconstruction ended after ten years in failure rather because of a change in public opinion in the North than because of the resistance of the Southern whites. The North of 1877, indeed, was not the North of 1867. A more tolerant attitude toward the South developed as the North passed through its own period of misgovernment when all the large cities were subject to "ring rule" and corruption, as in New York under "Boss" Tweed and in the District of Columbia under "Boss" Shepherd. The Federal civil service was discredited by the scandals connected with the Sanborn contracts, the Whisky Ring, and the Star Routes, while some leaders in Congress were under a cloud from the "Salary Grab" and Credit Mobilier disclosures.[1]

---

[1] See *The Boss and the Machine,* by Samuel P. Orth (in *The Chronicles of America*).

The marvelous material development of the North and West also drew attention away from sectional controversies. Settlers poured into the plains beyond the Mississippi and the valleys of the Far West; new industries sprang up; unsuspected mineral wealth was discovered; railroads were built. Not only bankers but taxpaying voters took an interest in the financial readjustments of the time. Many thousand people followed the discussions over the funding and refunding of the national debt, the retirement of the greenbacks, and the proposed lowering of tariff duties. Yet the Black Friday episode of 1869, when Jay Gould and James Fisk cornered the visible supply of gold, and the panic of 1873 were indications of unsound financial conditions.

These new developments and the new domestic problems which they involved all tended to divert public thought from the old political issues arising out of the war. Foreign relations, too, began to take on a new interest. The *Alabama* claims controversy with England continued to hold the public attention until finally settled by the Geneva Arbitration in 1872. President Grant, as much of an expansionist as Seward, for two years (1869-71) tried to secure Santo Domingo or a part of it for an

American naval base in the West Indies. But the United States had race problems enough already and the Senate, led by Sumner, refused to sanction the acquisition. Relations with Spain were frequently strained on account of American filibustering expeditions to aid Cuban insurgents. Spain repeatedly charged the United States with laxness toward such violations of international law; and President Grant, seeing no other way out, recommended in 1869 and again in 1870 that the Cuban insurgents be recognized as belligerents, but still the Senate held back. The climax came in 1873, when the Spanish authorities in Cuba captured on the high seas the *Virginius*[1] with a filibustering expedition on board and executed fifty-three of the crew and passengers, among them eight Americans. For a time war seemed imminent, but Spain acted quickly and effected a peaceable settlement.

It became evident soon after 1867 that the issues involved in reconstruction were not in themselves sufficient to hold the North solidly Republican. Toward negro suffrage, for example, Northern public opinion was on the whole unfriendly. In 1867 the negro was permitted to vote only in New York

[1] See *The Path of Empire*, by Carl Russell Fish (in *The Chronicles of America*), p. 119.

and in New England, except in Connecticut.   Before 1869 negro suffrage was rejected in Connecticut, Wisconsin, Kansas, Ohio, Maryland, Missouri, Michigan, and Minnesota.   The Republicans in their national platform of 1868 went only so far as to say that, while negro suffrage was to be forced upon the South, it must remain a local question in the North.   The Border States rapidly lined up with the white South on matters of race, church, and politics.

It was not until 1874, however, that the changing opinion was made generally effective in the elections.   The skillfully managed radical organization held large majorities in every Congress from the Thirty-ninth to the Forty-third, and the electoral votes in 1868 and 1872 seemed to show that the conservation opposition was insignificant.   But these figures do not tell the whole story.   Even in 1864, when Lincoln won by nearly half a million, the popular vote was as eighteen to twenty-two, and four years later Grant, the most popular man in the United States, had a majority of only three hundred thousand over Seymour, and this majority and more came from the new negro voters.   Four years later with about a million negro voters available and an opposition not pleased with its own candidate, Grant's majority reached only seven hundred thousand. At no one time in elections did the North pronounce itself in favor of all the reconstruction policies. The break, signs of which were visible as early as 1869, came in 1874 when the Republicans lost control of the House of Representatives.

Strength was given to the opposition because of the dissatisfaction with President Grant, who knew little about politics and politicians. He felt that his Cabinet should be made up of personal friends, not of strong advisers, and that the military ideal of administration was the proper one. He was faithful but undiscriminating in his friendships and frequently chose as his associates men of vulgar tastes and low motives; and he showed a naïve love of money and an undisguised admiration for rich men such as Gould and Fisk. His appointees were often incompetent friends or relatives, and his cynical attitude toward civil service reform lost him the support of influential men. When forced by party exigencies to select first-class men for his Cabinet, he still preferred to go for advice to practical politicians. On the Southern question he easily fell under control of the radicals, who in order to retain their influence had only to convince

his military mind that the South was again in rebellion, and who found it easy to distract public
opinion from political corruption by "waving the
bloody shirt." Dissatisfaction with his Administration, it is true, was confined to the intellectuals,
the reformers, and the Democrats, but they were
strong enough to defeat him for a second term if
they could only be organized.

The Liberal Republican movement began in the
West about 1869 with demands for amnesty and
for reform, particularly in the civil service, and it
soon spread rapidly over the North. When it became certain that the "machine" would renomi-
nate Grant, the liberal movement became an anti-
Grant party. The "New Departure" Democrats
gave comfort and prospect of aid to the Liberal Republicans by declaring for a constructive, forward-
looking policy in place of reactionary opposition.
The Liberal chiefs were led to believe that the new
Democratic leaders would accept their platform
and candidates in order to defeat Grant. The
principal candidates for the Liberal Republican
nomination were Charles Francis Adams, Lyman
Trumbull, Gratz Brown, David Davis, and Horace
Greeley. Adams was the strongest candidate but
was jockeyed out of place and the nomination was

given to Horace Greeley, able enough as editor of the *New York Tribune* but impossible as a candidate for the presidency. The Democratic party accepted him as their candidate also, although he had been a lifelong opponent of Democratic principles and policies. But disgusted Liberals either returned to the Republican ranks or stayed away from the polls, and many Democrats did likewise. Under these circumstances the reëlection of Grant was a foregone conclusion. There was certainly a potential majority against Grant, but the opposition had failed to organize, while the Republican machine was in good working order, the negroes were voting, and the Enforcement Acts proved a great aid to the Republicans in the Southern States.

One good result of the growing liberal sentiment was the passage of an Amnesty Act by Congress on May 22, 1872. By statute and by the Fourteenth Amendment, Congress had refused to recognize the complete validity of President Johnson's pardons and amnesty proclamations, and all Confederate leaders who wished to regain political rights had therefore to appeal to Congress. During the Forty-first Congress (1869–71) more than three thousand Southerners were amnestied in order that they might hold office. These, however, were for the most part scalawags; the most respectable whites would not seek an amnesty which they could secure only by self-stultification.[1] It was the pressure of public opinion against white disfranchisement and the necessity for meeting the Liberal Republican arguments which caused the passage of the Act of 1872. By this act about 150,000 whites were reënfranchised, leaving out only about five hundred of the most prominent of the old régime, most of whom were never restored to citizenship. Both Robert E. Lee and Jefferson Davis died disfranchised.

How the Southern whites escaped from negro domination has often been told and may here be sketched only in outline. The first States regained

[1] The machinery of government and politics was all in radical hands — the carpetbaggers and scalawags, who were numerous enough to fill practically all the offices. These men were often able leaders and skillful managers, and they did not intend to surrender control; and the black race was obedient and furnished the votes. In 1868, with Virginia, Mississippi, Georgia, and Texas unrepresented, the first radical contingent in Congress from the South numbered 42, of whom 10 out of 12 senators and 26 out of 32 representatives were carpetbaggers. There were two lone conservative Congressmen. A few months later, in 1869, there were 64 radical representatives from the South, 20 senators and 44 members of the House of Representatives. In 1877 this number had dwindled to two senators and four representatives. The difference between these figures measures in some degree the extent of the undoing of reconstruction within the period of Grant's Administration.

from radicalism were those in which the negro population was small and the black vote large enough to irritate but not to dominate. Although Northern sentiment, excited by the stories of "Southern outrage," was then unfavorable, the conservatives of the South, by organizing a "white man's party" and by the use of Ku Klux methods, made a fight for social safety which they won nearly everywhere, and, in addition, they gained political control of several States — Tennessee in 1869, Virginia in 1869–1870, and North Carolina and Georgia in 1870. They almost won Louisiana in 1868 and Alabama in 1870, but the alarmed radicals came to the rescue of the situation with the Fifteenth Amendment and the Enforcement Laws of 1870–1871. With more troops and a larger number of deputy marshals it seemed that the radicals might securely hold the remaining States. Arrests of conservatives were numerous, plundering was at its height, the Federal Government was interested and was friendly to the new Southern rulers, and the carpetbaggers and scalawags feasted, troubled only by the disposition of their negro supporters to demand a share of the spoils. Although the whites made little gain from 1870 to 1874, the States already rescued became more firmly conservative;

white counties here and there in the black States voted out the radicals; a few more representatives of the whites got into Congress; and the Border States ranged themselves more solidly with the conservatives.

But while the Southern whites were becoming desperate under oppression, public opinion in the North was at last beginning to affect politics. The elections of 1874 resulted in a Democratic landslide of which the Administration was obliged to take notice. Grant now grew more responsive to criticism. In 1875 he replied to a request for troops to hold down Mississippi: "The whole public are tired out with these annual autumnal outbreaks in the South and the great majority are ready now to condemn any interference on the part of the Government." As soon as conditions in the South were better understood in the North, ready sympathy and political aid were offered by many who had hitherto acted with the radicals. The Ku Klux report as well as the newspaper writings and the books of J. S. Pike and Charles Nordhoff, both former opponents of slavery, opened the eyes of many to the evil results of negro suffrage. Some who had been considered friends of the negro, now believing that he had proven to be a political failure, coldly abandoned him and turned their altruistic interests to other objects more likely to succeed. Many real friends of the negro were alarmed at the evils of the reconstruction and were anxious to see the corrupt political leaders deprived of further influence over the race. To others the constantly recurring Southern problem was growing stale and they desired to hear less of it. Within the Republican party in each Southern State there were serious divisions over the spoils. First it was carpetbagger and negro against the scalawag; later, when the black leaders insisted that those who furnished the votes must have the larger share of the rewards, the fight became triangular. As a result, by 1874 the Republican party in the South was split into factions and was deserted by a large proportion of its white membership.

The conservative whites, fiercely resentful after their experiences under the enforcement laws and hopeful of Northern sympathy, now planned a supreme effort to regain their former power. Race lines were more strictly drawn; ostracism of all that was radical became the rule; the Republican party in the South, it was apparent, was doomed to be only a negro party weighed down by the scandal of bad government; the state treasuries were

bankrupt, and there was little further opportunity
for plunder.   These considerations had much to do
with the return of scalawags to the "white man's
party" and the retirement of carpetbaggers from
Southern politics.   There was no longer anything
in it, they said; let the negro have it!

It was under these conditions that the "white
man's party" carried the elections in Alabama,
Arkansas, and Texas in 1874, and Mississippi in
1875.   Asserting that it was a contest between civilization and barbarism, and that the whites under
the radical régime had no opportunity to carry an
election legally, the conservatives openly made use
of every method of influencing the result that could
possibly come within the radical law and they even
employed many effective methods that lay outside
the law.   Negroes were threatened with discharge
from employment and whites with tar and feathers
if they voted the radical ticket; there were night-
riding parties, armed and drilled "white leagues,"
and mysterious firing of guns and cannon at night;
much plain talk assailed the ears of the radical
leaders; and several bloody outbreaks occurred,
principally in Louisiana and Mississippi.   Louisiana had been carried by the Democrats in the
fall of 1872, but the radical returning board had

reversed the election.   In 1874 the whites rose in rebellion and turned out Kellogg, the usurping Governor, but President Grant intervened to restore him to office. The "Mississippi" or "shot-gun plan"[1] was very generally employed, except where the contest was likely to go in favor of the whites without the use of undue pressure.   The white leaders exercised a moderating influence, but the average white man had determined to do away with negro government even though the alternative might be a return of military rule.   Congress investigated the elections in each State which overthrew the reconstructionists, but nothing came of the inquiry and the population rapidly settled down into good order.   After 1875 only three States were left under radical government — Louisiana and Florida, where the returning boards could throw out any Democratic majority, and South Carolina, where the negroes greatly outnumbered the whites.

Reconstruction could hardly be a genuine issue in the presidential campaign of 1876, because all except these three reconstructed States had escaped from radical control, and there was no hope and

[1] See *The New South*, by Holland Thompson (in *The Chronicles of America*).

little real desire of regaining them. It was even expected that in this year the radicals would lose Louisiana and Florida to the "white man's party." The leaders of the best element of the Republicans, both North and South, looked upon the reconstruction as one of the prime causes of the moral breakdown of their party; they wanted no more of the Southern issue but planned a forward-looking, constructive reform.

To some of the Republican leaders, however, among whom was James G. Blaine, it was clear that the Republican party, with its unsavory record under Grant's Administration, could hardly go before the people with a reform program. The only possible thing to do was to revive some Civil War issue — "wave the bloody shirt" and fan the smoldering embers of sectional feeling. Blaine met with complete success in raising the desired issue. In January, 1876, when an amnesty measure was brought before the House, he moved that Jefferson Davis be excepted on the ground that he was responsible for the mistreatment of Union prisoners during the war. Southern hotbloods replied, and Blaine skillfully led them on until they had foolishly furnished him with ample material for campaign purposes. The feeling thus aroused was so strong that it even galvanized into seeming life the dying interest in the wrongs of the negro. The rallying cry "Vote as you shot!" gave the Republicans something to fight for; the party referred to its war record, claimed credit for preserving the Union, emancipating the negro, and reconstructing the South, and demanded that the country be not "surrendered to rebel rule."

Hayes and Tilden, the rival candidates for the presidency, were both men of high character and of moderate views. Their nominations had been forced by the better element of each party. Hayes, the Republican candidate, had been a good soldier, was moderate in his views on Southern questions, and had a clean political reputation. Tilden, his opponent, had a good record as a party man and as a reformer, and his party needed only to attack the past record of the Republicans. The principal Democratic weakness lay in the fact that the party drew so much of its strength from the white South and was therefore subjected to criticism on Civil War issues.

The campaign was hotly contested and was conducted on a low plane. Even Hayes soon saw that the "bloody shirt" issue was the main vote winner. The whites of the three "unredeemed" Southern

States nerved themselves for the final struggle. In South Carolina and in some parishes of Louisiana there was a considerable amount of violence, in which the whites had the advantage, and much fraud, which the Republicans, who controlled the election machinery, turned to best account. It has been said that out of the confusion which the Republicans created they won the presidency.

The first election returns seemed to give Tilden the victory with 184 undisputed electoral votes and popular majorities of ninety and over six thousand respectively in Florida and Louisiana; only 185 votes were needed for a choice. Hayes had 166 votes, not counting Oregon, in which one vote was in dispute, and South Carolina, which for a time was claimed by both parties. Had Louisiana and Florida been Northern States, there would have been no controversy, but the Republican general headquarters knew that the Democratic majorities in these States had to go through Republican returning boards, which had never yet failed to throw them out.

The interest of the nation now centered around the action of the two returning boards. At the suggestion of President Grant, prominent Republicans went South to witness the count. Later prominent Democrats went also. These "visiting statesmen" were to support the frail returning boards in their duty. It was generally understood that these boards, certainly the one in Louisiana, were for sale, and there is little doubt that the Democrats inquired the price. But they were afraid to bid on such uncertain quantities as Governor Wells and T. C. Anderson of Louisiana, both notorious spoilsmen. The members of the boards in both States soon showed the stiffening effect of the moral support of the Federal Administration and of the "visiting statesmen." Reassured as to their political future, they proceeded to do their duty: in Florida they threw out votes until the ninety majority for Tilden was changed to 925 for Hayes, and in Louisiana, by throwing out about fifteen thousand carefully selected ballots, they changed Tilden's lowest majority of six thousand to a Hayes majority of nearly four thousand. Naturally the Democrats sent in contesting returns, but the presidency was really won when the Republicans secured in Louisiana and Florida returns which were regular in form. But hoping to force Congress to go behind the returns, the Democrats carried up contests also from Oregon and South Carolina, whose votes properly belonged to Hayes.

The final contest came in Congress over the counting of the electoral votes. The Constitution provides that "the President of the Senate shall, in the presence of the Senate and the House of Representatives, open all the Certificates, and the Votes shall then be counted." But there was no agreement as to where authority lay for deciding disputed votes. Never before had the presidency turned on a disputed count. From 1864 to 1874 the "twenty-second joint rule" had been in force under which either House might reject a certificate. The votes of Georgia in 1868 and of Louisiana in 1872 had thus been thrown out. But the rule had not been readopted by the present Congress, and the Republicans very naturally would not listen to a proposal to readopt it now.

With the country apparently on the verge of civil war, Congress finally created by law an Electoral Commission to which were to be referred all disputes about the counting of votes and the decision of which was to be final unless both Houses concurred in rejecting it. The act provided that the commission should consist of five senators, five representatives, four designated associate justices of the Supreme Court, and a fifth associate justice to be chosen by these four. While nothing was said in the act about the political affiliations of the members of the commission, every one understood that the House would select three Democrats and two Republicans, and that the Senate would name two Democrats and three Republicans. It was also well known that of the four justices designated two were Republicans and two Democrats, and it was tacitly agreed that the fifth would be Justice David Davis, an "independent." But at the last moment Davis was elected Senator by the Illinois Legislature and declined to serve on the Commission. Justice Bradley, a Republican, was then named as the fifth justice, and in this way the Republicans obtained a majority on the Commission.

The Democrats deserve the credit for the Electoral Commission. The Republicans did not favor it, even after they were sure of a party majority on it. They were conscious that they had a weak case, and they were afraid to trust it to judges of the Supreme Court. Their fears were groundless, however, since all important questions were decided by an 8 to 7 vote, Bradley voting with his fellow Republicans. Every contested vote was given to Hayes, and with 185 electoral votes he was declared elected on March 2, 1877.

Ten years before, Senator Morton of Indiana had

said: "I would have been in favor of having the colored people of the South wait a few years until they were prepared for the suffrage, until they were to some extent educated, but the necessities of the times forbade that; the conditions of things required that they should be brought to the polls at once." Now the condition of things required that some arrangement be made with the Southern whites which would involve a complete reversal of the situation of 1867. In order to secure the unopposed succession of Hayes, to defeat filibustering which might endanger the decision of the Electoral Commission, politicians who could speak with authority for Hayes assured influential Southern politicians, who wanted no more civil war but who did want home rule, that an arrangement might be made which would be satisfactory to both sides.

So the contest was ended. Hayes was to be President; the South, with the negro, was to be left to the whites; there would be no further military aid to carpetbag governments. In so far as the South was concerned, it was a fortunate settlement — better, indeed, than if Tilden had been inducted into office. The remnants of the reconstruction policy were surrendered by a Republican President, the troops were soon withdrawn, and the three radical States fell at once under the control of the whites. Hayes could not see in his election any encouragement to adopt a vigorous radical position, and Congress was deadlocked on party issues for fifteen years. As a result the radical Republicans had to develop other interests, and the North gradually accepted the Southern situation.

Although the radical policy of reconstruction came to an end in 1877, some of its results were more lasting. The Southern States were burdened heavily with debt, much of which had been fraudulently incurred. There now followed a period of adjustment, of refunding, scaling, and repudiation, which not only injured the credit of the States but left them with enormous debts. The Democratic party under the leadership of former Confederates began its régime of strict economy, race fairness, and inelastic Jeffersonianism. There was a political rest which almost amounted to stagnation and which the leaders were unwilling to disturb by progressive measures lest a developing democracy make trouble with the settlement of 1877.

The undoing of reconstruction was not entirely completed with the understanding of 1877. There remained a large but somewhat shattered Republican party in the South, with control over county and local government in many negro districts. Little by little the Democrats rooted out these last vestiges of negro control, using all the old radical methods and some improvements,[1] such as tissue ballots, the shuffling of ballot boxes, bribery, force, and redistricting, while some regions were placed entirely under executive control and were ruled by appointed commissions. With the good government which followed these changes a deadlocked Congress showed no great desire to interfere. The Supreme Court came to the aid of the Democrats with decisions in 1875, 1882, and 1883 which drew the teeth from the Enforcement Laws, and Congress in 1894 repealed what was left of these regulations.

Under such discouraging conditions the voting strength of the Republicans rapidly melted away. The party organization existed for the Federal offices only and was interested in keeping down the number of those who desired to be rewarded. As a consequence, the leaders could work in harmony with those Democratic chiefs who were content with a "solid South" and local home rule. The negroes

[1] See *The New South*, by Holland Thompson (in *The Chronicles of America*).

of the Black Belt, with less enthusiasm and hope, but with quite the same docility as in 1868, began to vote as the Democratic leaders directed. This practice brought up in another form the question of "negro government" and resulted in a demand from the people of the white counties that the negro be put entirely out of politics. The answer came between 1890 to 1902 in the form of new and complicated election laws or new constitutions which in various ways shut out the negro from the polls and left the government to the whites. Three times have the Black Belt regions dominated the Southern States: under slavery, when the master class controlled; under reconstruction, when the leaders of the negroes had their own way; and after reconstruction until negro disfranchisement, when the Democratic dictators of the negro vote ruled fairly but not always acceptably to the white counties which are now the source of their political power.

BIBLIOGRAPHICAL NOTE

THE best general accounts of the reconstruction period
are found in James Ford Rhodes's *History of the United
States from the Compromise of 1850 to the Restoration of
Home Rule at the South in 1877*, volumes V, VI, VII (1906);
in William A. Dunning's *Reconstruction, Political and
Economic, 1865–1877*, in the *American Nation* Series,
volume XXII (1907); and in Peter Joseph Hamilton's *The
Reconstruction Period* (1905), which is volume XVI of *The
History of North America*, edited by F. N. Thorpe. The
work of Rhodes is spacious and fair-minded but there are
serious gaps in his narrative; Dunning's briefer account
covers the entire field with masterly handling; Hamilton's history throws new light on all subjects and is
particularly useful for an understanding of the Southern
point of view. A valuable discussion of constitutional
problems is contained in William A. Dunning's *Essay
on the Civil War and Reconstruction and Related Topics*
(1904); and a criticism of the reconstruction policies
from the point of view of political science and constitutional law is to be found in J. W. Burgess's *Reconstruction and the Constitution, 1866–1876* (1902). E. B. Andrews's *The United States in our own Time* (1903) gives
a popular treatment of the later period. A collection
of brief monographs entitled *Why the Solid South?* by
Hilary A. Herbert and others (1890) was written as a

campaign document to offset the drive made by the Republicans in 1889 for new enforcement laws.

There are many scholarly monographs on reconstruction in the several States. The best of these are: J. W. Garner's *Reconstruction in Mississippi* (1901), W. L. Fleming's *Civil War and Reconstruction in Alabama* (1905), J. G. deR. Hamilton's *Reconstruction in North Carolina* (1914), W. W. Davis's *The Civil War and Reconstruction in Florida* (1913), J. S. Reynolds's *Reconstruction in South Carolina, 1865–1877* (1905); C. W. Ramsdell's *Reconstruction in Texas* (1910), and C. M. Thompson's *Reconstruction in Georgia* (1915).

Books of interest on special phases of reconstruction are not numerous, but among those deserving mention are Paul S. Pierce's *The Freedmen's Bureau* (1904), D. M. DeWitt's *The Impeachment and Trial of Andrew Johnson* (1903), and Paul L. Haworth's *The Hayes-Tilden Disputed Presidential Election of 1876* (1906), each of which is a thorough study of its field. J. C. Lester and D. L. Wilson's *Ku Klux Klan* (1905) and M. L. Avary's *Dixie After the War* (1906) contribute much to a fair understanding of the feeling of the whites after the Civil War; and Gideon Welles, *Diary,* 3 vols. (1911), is a mine of information from a conservative cabinet officer's point of view.

For the politician's point of view one may go to James G. Blaine's *Twenty Years of Congress,* 2 vols. (1884, 1886) and Samuel S. Cox's *Three Decades of Federal Legislation* (1885). Good biographies are James A. Woodburn's *The Life of Thaddeus Stevens* (1913), Moorfield Storey's *Charles Sumner* (1900), C. F. Adams's *Charles Francis Adams* (1900). Less satisfactory because more partisan is Edward Stanwood's *James*

Gillespie Blaine (1906). There are no adequate biographies of the Democratic and Southern leaders.

The official documents are found conveniently arranged in William McDonald's *Select Statutes, 1861–1898* (1903), and also with other material in Walter L. Fleming's *Documentary History of Reconstruction*, 2 vols. (1906, 1907). The general reader is usually repelled by the collections known as *Public Documents*. The valuable *Ku Klux Trials* (1872) is, however, separately printed and to be found in most good libraries. By a judicious use of the indispensable *Tables and Index to Public Documents* one can find much vividly interesting material in connection with contested election cases and reports of congressional investigations into conditions in the South.

INDEX

Chase—*Continued*
advises Johnson against suspending Stanton, 163; and impeachment of Johnson, 166–67
Civil Rights Act, 84, 137, 141, 277
Clanton, General J. H., of Alabama, on position of whites, 250
Clayton, Judge, of Alabama, opinion of Freedmen's Bureau, 90
Clayton, Mrs., *Black and White under the Old Régime*, quoted, 38–39
Cleveland, soldiers' and sailors' convention at, 130; Union League formed (1862), 176–177
Clinton (Miss.), race conflict in, 237 (note)
Cloud, school official in Alabama, 216
Colfax, Schuyler, candidate for Vice President (1868), 168
Colfax (La.), race conflict in, 237 (note)
Columbia (S. C.), post-war condition, 5
Congress, impatient of executive precedence, 65–66, 119–20; and Southern representatives, 80, 86, 119–20, 128; refuses to recognize reconstructed governments, 81; Joint Committee on Reconstruction, 82, 84, 121, 125–26, 127, 129–30, 131, 198, 266 (note); Fourteenth Amendment, 82, 85, 130; *see also* Constitution; radical reconstruction plans, 83–84; radicalism, 83–84, 118 *et seq.*, 285; Civil Rights Act, 84, 137, 141, 277; and Johnson, 126 *et seq.*; assumes control of reconstruction, 129, 142–43; Tenure of Office Act, 134; Army Appropriation Act, 134; reconstruction acts, 134–37, 158–60; su-

preme control, 140; and Supreme Court, 158–59; impeachment of President, 160 *et seq.*; and Grant, 171; negro members, 230, 242; Committee on the Condition of the South, 241; Committee on the Late Insurrectionary States, 241; enforcement acts, 260, 261–62, 290, 292, 303; "Ku Klux Bill," 261, 262; committee to investigate conditions in Southern States, 262; Amnesty Act (1872), 288–89; decline of radicalism, 289 (note), 290; investigates election, 294; amnesty measure (1876), 295; Electoral Commission, 299–300; deadlocked by party issues, 302
Connecticut and negro suffrage, 285
Constitution, Johnson and, 72, 162; Thirteenth Amendment, 79; Fourteenth Amendment, 82, 84, 85, 130, 131–33, 135–136, 137, 156, 172; Fifteenth Amendment, 169–70, 171, 172, 222, 290
Constitutional conventions in South, 152 *et seq.*
Constitutional Union Guards, 245
Conway, school official in Louisiana, 216
Copperheads, 176
Cotton, tax on, 8; seized, 9–11; destruction of, 11; production (1880), 271–72 (note)
Council of Safety, 245
Coushatta (La.), race conflict in, 237 (note)
Cowan, administration Republican, 122
Credit Mobilier, 282
Crittenden-Johnson resolutions, 55, 69
Cuba, United States and, 284
Cumberland Presbyterian Church, 204

Richmond (Va.), post-war condition, 5; Halleck's order in regard to marriage, 20; incident of Lee and a negro in church, 43–44; Lincoln and Confederate Government in, 67

Rifle Clubs of South Carolina, 245–46, 263

Roads in Tennessee after Civil War, 4

Saffold, M. J., on negro suffrage, 50

"Salary Grab," 282

Santo Domingo, Grant seeks annexation of, 283–84

Savannah (Ga.), incident relating to Confederate uniforms, 20–21

Scalawags, in constitutional conventions, 153; desert radicals, 156; disabilities removed, 171; and the churches, 205; use of term, 222

Schofield, General J. M., 106; commands military district, 140 (note); Secretary of War, 167

Schuckers, J. W., quoted, 166

Schurz, Carl, on army of occupation, 19; report on conditions in South, 28, 29, 30; on negro labor, 45–46

Scott, R. K., Governor of South Carolina, 236

Sea Islands, negroes sent to, 36, 103, 114

Seward, W. H., and Jackson, 74; expansionist, 283

Seymour, Horatio, of New York, 168, 169

Sharkey, W. L., Governor of Mississippi, 78

Shepherd, A. R., 282

Shepley, General G. F., military governor of Louisiana, 65

Sheridan, General P. H., commands military district, 140–

141 (note); Johnson removes, 163; "banditti" report, 241

Sherman, General W. T., 28, 36; Sea Island order, 103, 114

Shot Gun Plan, see Mississippi Shot Gun Plan

Sickles, General D. E., commands military district, 140–41(note); removed by Johnson, 163

Slavery, Abolition of, Lincoln and, 58, 66; Johnson and, 58, 76; Sumner and, 59; see also Emancipation Proclamation

Smith, Gerrit, view of reconstruction, 60–61

Smith, W. H., Governor of Alabama, 207, 224; quoted, 24

Somers, Robert, English writer on the South, 4, 28–29, 41–42, 269

Sons of '76, 245

South, post-war condition, 2 et seq.; exploitation by Northerners, 26–27; relation between races, 47–48; Presidents' work of reconstruction, 54 et seq.; see also Reconstruction; conference of governors of, 85; military rule in, 140 et seq.; churches, 196–208; schools, 208–20; carpetbag and negro rule, 221 et seq.; social conditions, 265 et seq.

South Carolina, Pike's account of post-war condition, 16–17; negroes on Sea Islands of, 36; negro legislation, 94, 95, 96, 275, 276; negro voters, 151, 152, 222; race lines abolished, 154; schools, 215–16, 217; carpetbag rule, 221, 225; conservatives, 223; judiciary, 225; negroes in legislature of, 226, 227; taxes, 231; public debt, 232; corruption, 234; negro militia, 236; elections, 239, 297, 298; put under martial law, 261; labor, 267, 268; Irish in, 271; and radicalism, 294